*A Parent's Guide
to Teaching Children Mitzvot:
A Halakhic Guide*

A Parent's Guide to Teaching Children Mitzvot: A Halakhic Guide

by

Rabbi Shmuel Singer

Ktav Publishing House, Inc.
Hoboken, NJ
5751/1991

Copyright © 1991
by Shmuel Singer

Library of Congress Cataloging-in-Publication Data

Singer, Shmuel.
    A parent's guide to teaching children Mitzvot : a Halakhic guide / Shmuel Singer.
       p. cm.
    Includes bibliographical references and index.
    ISBN 0-88125-367-7. — ISBN 0-88125-368-5 (pbk.)
    1. Judaism—Customs and practices—Study and teaching (Elementary)
2. Commandments (Judaism)—Study and teaching (Elementary)
I. Title.
BM700.S52   1991
296.3'07—dc20   90-24822
                                                                       CIP

Manufactured in the United States of America

This book is dedicated
with love and affection
to my wife
Reva
without whose encouragement and help
it could never have been written.
And to our wonderful daughters
Tziporah and Gila
for whom it was developed and written
in the first instance.
May G-d grant them all the best
in their future endeavors
and experience in life.

                           Shmuel Singer

ישיבת רבנו יצחק אלחנן
RABBI ISAAC ELCHANAN THEOLOGICAL SEMINARY

Affiliate - Yeshiva University
2540 Amsterdam Avenue / New York, N.Y. 10033 / (212) 960-5344

ב"ה

October 25, 1990

I have read various selections from the work written by my honored acquaintance Rabbi Shmuel Singer on the subject of educating children in mitzvot and I have found it to be a worthy and very helpful book collected from the writings of the great Halachic authorities of the past. The author is well-known for his fear of G-d, Torah knowledge and exacting scholarship. He can be relied upon for producing authoritative Halachic works.

The subject of educating children is very dear before G-d. We find that the patriarch Abraham was called G-d's beloved because of his great dedication to insuring the proper chinuch of his household, as the Torah tells us in Bereshit 18:19. There is no doubt that this subject requires great wisdom. Those who study this book will certainly find much benefit in it. They will be encouraged and strengthened in fulfilling this important mitzvah.

Rabbi Hershel Schachter
Rosh Kollel, Yeshiva University

ישיבת רבנו יצחק אלחנן
RABBI ISAAC ELCHANAN THEOLOGICAL SEMINARY
Affiliate - Yeshiva University
2540 Amsterdam Avenue / New York, N.Y. 10033 / (212) 960-5344

ב"ה

יום ג' לס' לך לך, ד' חשון, שנת תשנ"א

עיינתי בכמה מקומות בגליונות ספרו של ידידי יקירי הרב החשוב כב' הר"ר שמואל סינגר, שיחי', בעניני חינוך הבנים, ומצאתיו ליקוט נחמד ומאוד מועיל — מלוקט מספרי גדולי הפוסקים, וכבר איתמחי גברא ביר"ש, בתורתו, ובדייקנותו, וחזקה על חבר וכו', וענין חינוך הבנים דבר חביב הוא מאוד לפני הקב"ה, דאברהם אבינו נקרא אוהבי רק מפני דבר זה, שהי' מדקדק מאוד בעניני חינוך בני ביתו, וכדכתיב בקרא, כי ידעתיו למען אשר יצוה את בניו ואת ביתו אחריו ללכת בדע ד' וכו', ובודאי יש בענין זה חכמה גדולה, והמעיינים בספר הזה בודאי ימצאו בו רוב תועלת, ויתעוררו ויזדרזו לדקדק יותר במצוה חביבה זו.

הכותב והחותם לכבוד התורה ולומדיה,

Contents

Preface — xiii

One: General Rules of Chinuch — 3

Two: Chinuch for Daily Mitzvot — 9
    Covering the Head
    Washing of Hands Upon Arising
    Tzitzit
    Tefillin
    Prayer
    Minyan and Synagogue Services
    Blessings Before and After Food
    Notes

Three: Chinuch for Shabbat — 24
    Preparations for Shabbat
    Lighting of Candles
    Kiddush
    Shabbat Meals
    Havdalah
    Forbidden Labor and Children
    Carrying on Shabbat
    Games and Toys
    Notes

Four: Chinuch for Festivals — 44
    Passover and Chametz Medication
    Food for Babies on Pesach
    Bedikat Chametz
    Erev Pesach
    The Seder
    Sefirat HaOmer
    The Three Weeks of Mourning
    Rosh Hashanah and Yom Kippur
    Sukkot

Chanukah
　　　Purim
　　　Yom Tov and Chol Hamoed
　　　Notes

Five: Chinuch for General Mitzvot　　　　　　　　74
　　　Kashruth: Non-Kosher Medicine
　　　Kashruth: Milk and Meat
　　　Dolls and Magic
　　　Haircutting and Clothing
　　　Vows
　　　Death and Mourning
　　　Yichud
　　　Tziniut
　　　Notes

Six: Chinuch and the Education of Children　　　94
　　　Teaching One's Son Torah
　　　Paying Tuition
　　　Age and Curriculum
　　　Torah Education for Girls
　　　Coeducation
　　　Teaching Secular Studies
　　　Teaching a Child a Livelihood
　　　Notes

Seven: The Care of Children and Halachah　　　111
　　　The Obligation to Provide for Children
　　　Charity and Children
　　　Nursing
　　　Diapers
　　　Diapers on Shabbat and Yom Tov
　　　Children's Body Care on Shabbat and Yom Tov
　　　Food Preparation on Shabbat and Yom Tov
　　　Transporting a Child
　　　Medical Care of Children
　　　Babysitters and Teachers

Blessing Children
Notes

Eight: Chinuch and Special Children   138
General Principles
The Contemporary Deaf-Mute
The Mentally Deficient
Adopted Children
Notes

Nine: Bar and Bat Mitzvah   150
Halachic Adulthood
Adulthood and Bar and Bat Mitzvah
The Date of the Bar or Bat Mitzvah
Bar Mitzvah Ceremony
Bat Mitzvah
Conclusion
Notes

Preface

Throughout the ages of Jewish existence, having children and bringing them up properly have been central concerns for the religious Jew. It was always the hope and wish of Jewish adults that they would be granted the privilege of raising their sons and daughters to be faithful members of our people. This, of course, continues to be the case today. In the final analysis, there can be no greater source of pleasure for a person than the knowledge that he has succeeded in the difficult task of raising his children in this way.

As is common with other areas of life, Halachah codifies the guidelines to be followed by parents in reaching this goal. It is not sufficient to merely have good intentions when raising one's children. Detailed prescriptions and rules exist as to how the observant Jew should go about fulfilling this obligation. Chinuch, teaching children the observance of mitzvot, is regarded by Halachah as a serious religious obligation. To raise their children properly, Jewish parents must be familiar with the halachic rules governing this area of life. Using such knowledge they can then succeed in the awesome task of bringing up a new loyal generation for the Jewish people.

Unfortunately, the laws concerning the raising of children are not codified or organized in one central treatment, as is the case with many other halachic subjects, but are scattered through the four sections of the *Shulchan Aruch*. Even more remarkably, no later authority seems to have authored a work on the halachot of chinuch. In consequence, it is very difficult for parents to gain adequate knowledge of this important subject. Even those who are trained in Torah learning and capable of studying it on their own, using the original halachic sources, might find the undertaking onerous. Those who lack sufficient Torah svolarship would find it even more difficult to learn what they need to know in this vital area of life.

I became aware of this situation while serving as a congregational rabbi for a number of years. Questions on the halachic raising of children were among the most common queries I received. It was while I researched the answers to these queries that it became apparent to me that no comprehensive halachic treatment of childrearing existed. The necessity for a work on the subject became clear, especially after my wife and I were blessed with our own children; my personal needs reinforced my belief that such a sefer was needed.

In today's Jewish community we have had the merit of seeing an ever increasing number of young people resolving to live their lives as religious and observant Jews. These people, of course, go on to begin families and raise children. Their need for a work devoted to the halachic ramifications of teaching children mitzvot and raising them as faithful Jews is obvious.

This work does not attempt to be the final word on the subject. An earnest attempt has been made to go through the entire spectrum of Halachah and discuss all the questions which relate to the subject of teaching children to observe mitzvot and raising them as religious Jews. Certain rarely occurring and extremely complicated issues have not been discussed. I have included a chapter on special children since this topic is increasingly of concern to the observant community today. The book is meant to provide a framework for the study and discussion of the subject of chinuch. In many cases I have merely quoted the different opinions which exist about certain issues without attempting to indicate which view should be followed. The reader is invited to discuss such matters with a competent rabbinic authority. The same is true in regard to issues which remain unclear to the reader after completing this book. In all such cases competent rabbinic advice and direction are called for.

I would like to express my thanks to Dr. Yaakov Elman of Ktav Publishing House, whose suggestions and advice have been most helpful in bringing this work to its completion. Without his thoughtful contributions it is doubtful whether this sefer would ever have seen the light of day. I also want to thank Katherine Couto, my secretary while I served as rabbi in Providence, Rhode Island, for her willingness to type the entire manuscript of this book and make the many corrections necessary in it. Her cheerful disposition and unfailing desire to help were most important in bringing about the completion of this work.

Finally and most significantly, I wish to express my deep gratitude to my wife Reva for her constant inspiration and encouragement in the writing of this sefer. Without her, this book would never have been begun in the first place, and certainly would not have been completed. As the model of a true Jewish mother, she provided me with an example of chinuch in action worthy of being emulated. Her halachic questions and suggestions formed the core and backbone of this work. In a true sense this sefer is every bit as much hers as it is mine.

It is my earnest prayer that this work may provide halachic guidance, in at least some small way, to parents seeking to fulfill the serious religious duty of chinuch towards their children. If it succeeds in helping parents to raise their sons and daughters as religious Jews in a halachically correct manner, then the time and effort this sefer has required will have been proven worthwhile. It is my prayer that, in the merit of the study of Torah and observance of mitzvot engendered by this work, my wife and I will be privileged to raise our children to be faithful members of the Jewish people. The *zechut* of having been granted such wonderful children served as the spur for much of the research behind this work. May we have the merit to see Tziporah Feiga and Gila Sara be a source of joy and inspiration to their parents, grandparents, and Klal Yisrael.

*A Parent's Guide
to Teaching Children Mitzvot:
A Halakhic Guide*

Chapter One

General Rules of Chinuch

Throughout the ages, chinuch, the religious training of children, has been one of the central concerns of Jewish parents. Parents have been willing to sacrifice much time and energy for this goal. Places of residence, types of occupation, and many other important decisions have always been made with this factor in mind. The importance given to chinuch was not determined by emotional feeling alone. It is a halachically binding requirement on Jewish parents to train their children to observe mitzvot and grow up to be religiously observant Jewish adults. A faithful Jew can no more neglect this law than he can violate any other precept of Halachah. It is a parent's God-given duty to see to it that this goal is accomplished.

The classic works of Judaism expand on the great importance of children being brought up religiously in order to carry on the heritage of our faith. The Midrash, in one well-known passage, states that when the Jewish people stood at Mount Sinai to receive the Torah, they were asked by God for a guarantee that they would indeed observe the Torah in the future. The only security which God was willing to accept, concludes the Midrash, was the children of the Jewish people. Through them, God could be certain that the Torah would be preserved among His people.[1] This passage highlights the overwhelming significance of chinuch in the Jewish scheme of things.

The general duty of chinuch refers to the obligation on the part of parents to educate their children to observe mitzvot. This means training children to perform positive mitzvot, which involve doing specifically required actions, as well as educating them to avoid violating negative mitzvot, which forbid the performance of certain acts. This obligation is obviously of great importance, as it ensures the future survival of the Torah among the Jewish people. Despite this, the duty to train children in mitzvah observance is not of Torah origin. Indeed, it is not a Torah requirement at all, but is rabbinic in nature. The Talmud states that whatever an adult is required to do by Torah law, a minor is obligated to fulfill by rabbinic decree.[2]

This statement, in the first instance, creates a requirement for parents to see to it that their children observe mitzvot. The children themselves are minors and therefore exempt from mitzvah observance on their own, as far as Torah law is concerned. Nevertheless, parents are rabbinically obligated to make sure that their children observe the Torah, so that they will be accustomed to doing this when they reach the age of adulthood.[3] This requirement is connected by the rabbis to the verse in the Book of Proverbs which states, "Teach a child according to his way so that even when he becomes old he will not turn from it."[4]

There are Rishonim who argue not only that parents of a minor are obligated to educate him to observe mitzvot, but that the minor himself is rabbinically required to do the same. In other words, rabbinic law creates an independent obligation on minors themselves to observe all the mitzvot of the Torah. This is separate and distinct from the duty of chinuch which falls on their parents. Other Rishonim disagree. They state that the duty of chinuch rest only on the parents of a minor. The child is not obligated to do anything in regard to mitzvot. The reasoning behind this is that, by definition, a minor is not an adult. Since this is so, he cannot be halachically obligated to perform any action on his own. Only his parents can be so obligated.[5]

The Talmud in its discussion of chinuch only refers to a *katan*, or male child. It does not mention the requirements of parents towards a daughter. There appear to be contradictory statements in the Talmud about whether or not there is an obligation of chinuch in regard to girls.[6] The conclusion of the poskim is that the obligation of chinuch is the same for boys as for girls.[7]

Similarly, the Talmud refers only to the obligation of chinuch which rests on the father of a child. It does not clearly state that such a duty is binding on the mother. Some poskim argue that mothers have no such halachic obligation.[8] Others debate the point. They say that we should assume that mothers have the same duty of chinuch as do fathers.[9] *Magen Avraham* agrees with the first view. He writes that only a father has the obligation of chinuch.[10] The majority of later poskim, however, disagree with *Magen Avraham*. They recommend that one follow the view that mothers are obligated by the duty of chinuch to train their children in mitzvot just as fathers are.[11]

There is no uniform time at which the duty of training a child to observe mitzvot begins. Mitzvot are divided into two main categories. The first of these comprise the *mitzvot asei*, or positive commandments; these require a person to perform specific actions in order to fulfill his or her religious duty. It is clear that parents are not obligated to see to it that their children observe the positive mitzvot as infants.[12] The requirement of chinuch comes into effect when the child is old enough to understand and perform the mitzvah he is being taught to observe. Only when the child has attained the requisite degree of intellectual maturity do parents have to start accustoming him to follow the particular mitzvah involved. In effect, this means that the age at which chinuch should begin for any mitzvah may differ from child to child. Children who have reached the age of five or six are, on the average, usually at the required stage of maturity. Their parents, therefore, have the duty of training them to observe these mitzvot.[13] However, every child is not necessarily included in this general rule. Certain children may not yet have reached this stage by the age of five or six. In the final analysis, the parent's obligation will always depend on the specific observance and the intellectual ability of the child concerned.[14]

The second category of mitzvot is made up of the negative commandments. These mitzvot involve actions which a Jew is forbidden to do. The duty of chinuch obligates parents to ensure that their children observe these mitzvot, just as they must see to it that they fulfill the positive commandments. This means that if a child attempts to perform a forbidden action and thus to violate Jewish law, his parents are required to stop him from doing so. The duty of chinuch makes the parents responsible for such actions of their child.[15] The parental obligation to stop the child from spontaneously violating mitzvot applies equally to Torah prohibitions and to rabbinic ones. In both cases the parent is required by the duty of chinuch to see that the child refrains from violating halachic restrictions.[16]

Parents become liable to fulfill this requirement of chinuch from the time that their child is old enough to understand that a particular action is wrong or prohibited. Again, the age is not a uniform one. It will depend on the prohibition and the intellectual maturity of the child.[17] As a general rule, the requisite level will be reached earlier than the age at which parents have to begin teaching their children to observe positive commandments. This is because it is not necessary for the child to be able to perform any action in regard to negative mitzvot. All that is required is that the child be able to understand that a certain act is wrong.[18] Most children reach this level of maturity somewhere during their preschool years.

There is yet a third category of mitzvot affected by the parental duty of chinuch. The Torah forbids a Jewish adult to order a child or cause him in any way to violate any halachic prohibition. It is rabbinically prohibited to do the same in regard to any rabbinic law. This restriction actually applies to all Jewish adults and not only to parents, though parents are the ones mostly affected by it. The prohibition of causing a child to sin begins from the time of the child's birth. Thus it is far more inclusive than the rules of chinuch, which concern accustoming a child to fulfill positive or negative mitzvot on his own. The difference here is that the parent or other adult is the active agent causing the child to sin. This prohibition is not restricted to direct involvement in causing the child to violate Halachah. Placing forbidden food in front of a child who is likely to eat it is also considered to be prohibited by this law. It is not necessary to actually feed the food to the child in order to violate this law.[19]

General Rules of Chinuch   7

It must be noted that there is a second opinion in regard to this question. Some Rishonim hold that a parent is permitted to directly cause a child to violate a rabbinic prohibition if he does so for the benefit of the child. It is, however, forbidden to cause a child to violate such restrictions when the violation is for the sake of someone other than the child. According to this view, parents also are not bound by the duty of chinuch to stop their children from transgressing a rabbinic prohibition on their own, as long as the child is doing this action for his own benefit. All of this is only true in regard to rabbinic prohibitions but not for Torah laws.[20] This view is not quoted in the *Shulchan Aruch*.[21] Nonetheless, many later poskim allow parents to rely on this opinion.[22] Other authorities state that parents should only follow the lenient view in cases of great necessity.[23]

In addition to ensuring that their children observe mitzvot, parents have a further teaching responsibility towards their offspring. They are required to teach their children proper religious behavior and good character traits. Parents must bring up their sons and daughters to love and fear God and aspire towards holiness and sanctity. This training should begin at the earliest age possible. The sages state that a child still in the cradle benefits from exposure to an atmosphere of Torah learning and observance. They attribute the later spiritual accomplishments of important Jewish leaders to such exposure.[24] Indeed, in another connection the Talmud indicates that anti-halachic influences on a fetus in the womb can have a decisive effect on the child's future spiritual development as an adult.[25]

Included in this obligation is the responsibility of parents to bring up their children not to lie or to speak slander against others.[26] In addition, parents should see to it that their children not hear songs or music of a suggestive nature even in their earliest years.[27] The poskim further caution parents against frightening children by telling them that a cat, dog, or any other animal will take them away as a punishment. Such warnings are the opposite of the ethical Jewish atmosphere in which a child must be raised.[28] The Talmud states that parents should never promise a child something and not fulfill it, as this will only encourage the child to lie in later life. Training for ethical living must begin in childhood.[29]

Notes

1. מדרש שיר השירים רבה, א׳, ד׳.
2. חגיגה, דף ו׳, עמוד א׳.
3. רש״י שם, ד״ה "קטן מבעיא".
4. משלי כ״ב, ו׳, חיי אדם, כלל ס״ו, סעיף א׳.
5. תוספות, ד״ה "עד שיאכל", ברכות, דף מ״ח, עמוד א׳, פירוש הר״ן על הרי״ף, מגילה, דף י״ט, עמוד ב׳.
6. נזיר דף כ״ט, עמוד א׳, יומא דף פ״ב, עמוד א׳.
7. מגן אברהם, סימן שמ״ג, ס״ק א׳, מחצית השקל שם, משנה ברורה שם, ס״ק ב׳
8. תוספות שאנץ יומא מובא בתרומת הדשן, סימן צ״ד.
9. תרומת הדשן, סימן צ״ד.
10. מגן אברהם, סימן שמ״ג, ס״ק ב׳, מחצית השקל שם.
11. חיי אדם, כלל ס״ו, סעיף ב׳, משנה ברורה, סימן שמ״ג, ס״ק ב׳
12. מהא דשמאי משנה, סוכה דף כ״ח, עמוד א׳, ובגמרא שם, דף כ״ח, עמוד ב׳.
13. פרי מגדים, פתיחה כוללת לאורח חיים, חלק ב׳, ס״ק י׳.
14. מגן אברהם, סימן שמ״ג, ס״ק ג׳, משנה ברורה שם, ס״ק ג׳, ד׳.
15. אורח חיים, סימן שמ״ג.
16. משנה תורה, הלכות מאכלות אסורות, פרק י״ז, הלכה כ״ז.
17. משנה ברורה, סימן שמ״ג, ס״ק ג׳.
18. חיי אדם, כלל ס״ו, סעיף ג׳.
19. משנה ברורה, סימן שמ״ג, ס״ק ג׳, ד׳.
20. שו״ת הרשב״א חלק א׳, סימן צ״ב, פירוש הר״ן על הרי״ף בתחילת יומא.
21. אורח חיים, סימן שמ״ג.
22. מגן אברהם שם, ס״ק ג׳, ביאור הלכה שם, ד״ה "מדברי סופרים".
23. חיי אדם, כלל ס״ו, סעיף ו׳.
24. תפארת ישראל על מסכת אבות, פרק ב׳, משנה ח׳, ילקוט שמעוני, בראשית כ״ו, ל״ה.
25. יומא דף פ״ב, עמוד ב׳.
26. משנה ברורה, סימן שמ״ג, ס״ק ג׳.
27. אורח חיים, סימן תק״ס, שער הציון שם, ס״ק כ״ה.
28. שולחן ערוך הגרש״ז, הלכות שמירת הגוף והנפש, סעיף י״ב, קיצור שולחן ערוך, סימן ל״ג, סעיף י״ד.
29. סוכה דף מ״ו, עמוד ב׳.

Chapter Two

Chinuch for Daily Mitzvot

The life of the Jew is marked by observances which serve as signposts meant to continually direct one's attention to God and His Torah. Through these actions we are able to sanctify our lives and infuse holiness even into our seemingly mundane activities. One basic group of obligations concerns the behavior of the Jew in the course of ordinary daily life. These include the requirements of keeping one's head covered (if a male), washing one's hands on arising in the morning, wearing tzitzit and tefillin, daily prayer, and the making of berachot before and after eating. It is obvious that chinuch for children includes these basic practices. It is, however, necessary for each Jewish parent to decide when and how his child should be trained in these daily observances.

Covering the Head

The wearing of a headcovering by Jewish males is one of the most basic of daily observances. Indeed, it is often used today to distingush between observant Jewish men and others. Toddlers and small children often offer great resistance to this practice, and as a result parents find it difficult to get their young boys to wear head coverings. It is therefore necessary to determine the halachic status of this practice in order to know at what age parents are required to begin enforcing it.

Contrary to popular belief, covering the head at all times is not mandatory according to all halachic opinions. A substantial group of poskim claim that Halachah requires only that the head be covered during times of prayer. At all other times it is a *midat chasidut*, a pious practice, to have the head covered. One is, of course, encouraged to fulfill this practice, but it is not binding in the sense of a halachic requirement.[1] The *Taz*, however, argues that nowadays the situation has changed. Since going bareheaded has become a Christian practice, a Jew who does this is violating the Torah prohibition of *bechukoteihem lo telechu*, not to conduct oneself according to the practices of the non-Jews. Consequently, according to this opinion there is today a Torah prohibition against going bareheaded.[2] The Sephardic poskim do not accept the opinion of the *Taz*,[3] but some of the later Ashkenazic authorities do.[4] Contemporary Ashkenazic poskim do not give an unconditional answer to this question. They agree that one should attempt to follow the opinion of the *Taz*; however, when necessary they allow one to rely on the lenient view and go bareheaded.[5]

If we accept the logic of the *Taz*, parents would be required to stop their male children from going bareheaded, just as they must restrain their children from violating any *lo ta'aseh*. This obligation would begin at the age when the child can understand that going without a head covering is forbidden. According to the first opinion, however, it would appear that no such parental obligation exists. This is especially true since the Talmud itself implies that it was customary for boys to go bareheaded.[6] Nevertheless, *Magen Avraham*, who quotes this talmudic proof, advises that parents should accustom boys to have their heads covered while young. This is so that they will be imbued with the fear of God from an early age.[7] Thus, whether or not one regards this as an outright halachic obligation, it remains the correct thing to do.

Washing of Hands Upon Arising

The first thing a Jew is required to do upon arising is to wash his hands in the prescribed manner and make the blessing of *al netilat yadaim*. This obligation is a positive rabbinic duty.[8] It applies equally to men and women.[9] Since this is so, it appears obvious that parents are required to train children of either sex to wash their hands in the morning just as adults do. The poskim do indeed prescribe that this be done.[10] In this sense the requirement in regard to washing would be no different from the obligation of chinuch for any other positive commandment of rabbinic origin. Parents would be required to train children to wash their hands in the morning from the time that the child is capable of understanding the obligation. There is, however, a secondary point here. Washing one's hands in the morning has the additional mystical significance of removing *ru'ach ra'ah*, a harmful aura, from one's hands. According to this view, food that has been touched by unwashed hands should not be eaten. Since children touch food even before the age of chinuch, this opinion requires them to have their hands washed from as early an age as possible. In line with this approach, Rabbi Shneur Zalman of Liadi considers it meritorious to wash a baby boy's hands every morning from the time of circumcision onwards. However, he admits that the general practice is not in accordance with this.[11] This opinion is not quoted by other poskim.

Tzitzit

The wearing of tzitzit on the part of males is the fulfillment of a direct Torah law. Since this is so, parents clearly have the obligation of teaching their sons to observe this mitzvah, but since women are exempt from this obligation, there is no such duty in regard to girls.

At what age must one begin to accustom the child to the wearing of tzitzit? The Talmud states that a father has the obligation to obtain tzitzit for his son from the time that the boy knows how to cover himself properly with the tzitzit.[12] The Rema defines covering oneself properly as meaning knowing how to put two of the four tzitzit in front of oneself and two in the back, as well as being capable of holding the tzitzit in one's hand during the Shema.[13]

From the context of this discussion it is clear that the term tzitzit being used here refers to the talit, worn during prayers, rather than to the talit katan, worn under the shirt all day. This would mean that boys of elementary school age should be trained to wear the talit during Shachrit prayers just as adults do. This indeed is the contemporary custom of both the Sephardic and Western European Ashkenazic communities.[14] According to the Eastern European Ashkenazic practice, men do not wear the talit during prayers until they are married. This custom is based on the opinion of Maharil.[15] While this view is criticized by some later authorities,[16] it is defended by others.[17] Since the custom is for the talit katan to be worn all day under the shirt, the debate about the talit gadol worn during prayers is not that relevant. Even those who hold to this custom fulfill the requirement of chinuch by training children to wear the talit katan. Even those who do train boys to wear the talit during prayers distinguish between them and married adults. While married males are encouraged to cover their heads with the talit throughout the prayers, children and unmarried adults are not.[18]

As mentioned earlier, all authorities agree that boys should be trained to wear the talit katan throughout the day. Again, the correct age would be whenever the individual child is able to understand the mitzvah. Many Acharonim state that the contemporary custom is to begin the wearing of tzitzit at the age of three for all boys.[19] There are, however, those who do not require tzitzit until the age of six or seven at the earliest, depending on the particular child.[20] A further point should be noted. Normally speaking, the talit katan must be of a halachically correct size in order to enable an adult to fulfill the mitzvah of tzitzit by wearing it. The dimensions required are that the garment be large enough to cover the head and the major part of the body of an average nine-year-old. It is obvious that a talit katan of this size[21] cannot be used for a young child. The poskim state that the garment used by a young boy should be large enough to cover his head and the major part of his body. If the garment is smaller than this, the child should not be taught to make a blessing over the tzitzit.[22]

Tefillin

The requirement of wearing tefillin is also the fulfillment of a positive Torah duty, but has a completely different requirement than does the mitzvah of tzitzit. This is because tefillin bear the name of God and have an intrinsic holiness. Due to their sanctity, a person wearing tefillin must avoid entering unclean places or engaging in secular activities.[23] In line with this, the Talmud states that a father is required to train his minor son to put on tefillin when the boy is old enough to treat them in accordance with their special holiness.[24] Thus, according to Rabbi Yosef Caro, the proper time at which to begin training the child to wear tefillin depends on his maturity.[25] The Rema, however, agrees with the opinion of the Ba'al HaIttur that no minor under the age of thirteen should wear tefillin.[26] Below this age, it appears, we cannot rely on a child to treat the tefillin with proper holiness. The *Magen Avraham* agrees with Rema but states that the contemporary custom is for a boy to begin wearing tefillin two or three months prior to his thirteenth birthday. In this way the child becomes accustomed to the mitzvah.[27]

Many authorities disagree; they encourage the wearing of tefillin from an earlier age. The *Bach* states that a boy should begin fulfilling this mitzvah from the time that he begins studying Talmud.[28] *Pri Megadim* leans towards this view and adds that certainly from the age of twelve a minor should be taught to put on tefillin. The Chofetz Chaim agrees.[29] There are, however, poskim who hold with the more restrictive view and discourage the wearing of tefillin for any period of time prior to the actual bar mitzvah.[30] The prevailing practice in the contemporary Ashkenazic community is to follow the view of *Magen Avraham* and permit the boy to begin wearing tefillin a short time before his thirteenth birthday.[31] Of course, there are those who follow the other viewpoints. In some communities it was customary for an orphan to begin wearing tefillin a full year before his bar mitzvah. This was regarded as a special merit for his deceased parents.

Though the majority view of the poskim is to discourage this practice, a minority opinion does support it.[32] The Sephardic poskim, disagreeing with Rema and *Magen Avraham*, and following Rabbi Yosef Caro, consider tefillin to be no different from any other mitzvah. According to this approach, a boy should be trained to observe this obligation from the time that he is able to understand it and follow it properly, no matter what his age is.[33]

Prayer

A question often asked by parents is when to start teaching their child to pray. A secondary part of this query asks what prayers one must teach minor children to say. In order to give a halachic answer to this question we must distinguish between the various parts of the ordinary prayers. The first section of the Shachrit morning service is the Pesukai DeZimra, extending from Baruch She'amar to Yishtabach. This is followed by Shema and its blessings. The third part of the service is the Shemoneh Esreh. Each of these sections must be examined separately.

The only part of the entire prayer service that constitutes the fulfillment of a Torah obligation is the recitation of the Shema. It would seem obvious that parents are required by the obligation of chinuch to teach their children to fulfill this mitzvah. This, however, is not the case. There is an argument among the early authorities about just this point. Rashi claims that there is a special exemption from chinuch for the mitzvah of Shema, while Rabbenu Tam says that no such exemption exists.[34] It should be noted that whatever is true of the actual paragraphs of the Shema also holds true for the blessings of the Shema, berachot Keriyat Shema, which precede and follow the actual words of the Shema.[35] The *Shulchan Aruch* recommends that one follow the opinion of Rabbenu Tam, who says that the obligation of chinuch does apply to the mitzvah of Shema.[36] This would mean that a boy from approximately the age of six or seven should be taught to say the Shema and its blessings both in the morning and the evening.[37]

Since the saying of Shema is a positive mitzvah dependent on time (*mitzvah aseh shehazeman gerama*), women are exempt from it.[38] Since this is so, there is certainly no requirement to educate girls to observe this mitzvah as a fulfillment of chinuch. However, the *Shulchan Aruch* states that, despite this exemption, women are advised to say the beginning of the Shema as a sign of personally accepting God's sovereignty in their lives. It is unclear whether this means only the first verse of the Shema or the entire first paragraph.[39] In addition, it is true that both women and girls can voluntarily assume this mitzvah obligation, just as they can accept other nonbinding mitzvot.[40] This is the basis for the contemporary practice in most girls' schools for the students to recite the Shema and its blessings every morning.

The central part of the liturgy is, of course, the Shemoneh Esreh prayer. It is clear that there is no exemption for minors from this obligation. Boys are required to be educated to recite the Shemoneh Esreh three times a day, just as they must be taught to fulfill all other mitzvot. They would be obligated to do so from elementary school age onwards.[41]

There exists, however, a question as to whether parents are obligated to accustom girls to recite the Shemoneh Esreh at its stated times. This is due to the broader controversy as to whether women in general have a requirement to pray the Shemoneh Esreh three times a day. The opinion of Rambam is that women are only obligated to recite a prayer of some sort once a day. They are not required to recite the ordained words of the Shemoneh Esreh thrice daily. Ramban disagrees and claims that women have the exact same obligation in regard to the Shemoneh Esreh as do men. *Magen Avraham* discusses this controversy and notes that the prevailing practice is to follow the Rambam's opinion and *not* require women to say the three daily Shemoneh Esreh prayers. However, he personally recommends that women accept the stricter opinion of Ramban.[42] The *Mishnah Berurah* concurs with *Magen Avraham* and advises that women say both the Shachrit and Minchah Shemoneh Esreh,[43] while the *Aruch HaShulchan* states that the prevailing custom is for women to be lenient in accordance with Rambam's opinion.[44] The conclusion in regard to educating girls to recite the Shemoneh Esreh depends on these different opinions. If we accept the position of Ramban, as advised by *Magen Avraham*, then girls should be taught to say at least the Shachrit and Minchah Shemoneh Esreh. They can be excused from reciting the Maariv Shemoneh Esreh since that prayer is halachically less binding than the previous two. If, however, we rely on the Rambam's opinion, supported by *Aruch HaShulchan*, it would be sufficient to teach girls to pray once a day in some manner. Again this obligation would apply from the age of elementary school, at which point girls become capable of understanding this mitzvah.

The third part of the Shachrit service is the introductory Pesukai DeZimra. This section of Shachrit is meant as a prologue to the words of the Shemoneh Esreh. It therefore has the halachic status of the latter prayer. Whatever is true in regard to training children to say the Shemoneh Esreh will be equally true for teaching them to say Pesukai DeZimra.[45]

One last point should be made about children and prayer. Even though adults are forbidden to eat before Shachrit unless absolutely necessary, this is not true for children. Despite the fact that parents are required to see to it that their children fulfill the obligation of prayer, they still may give their children breakfast before they recite the Shachrit prayers.[46]

Minyan and Synagogue Services

Even though the Jew can fulfill his obligation of prayer on an individual basis, the Halachah strongly recommends that he pray with a minyan of at least ten adult males whenever possible. A minyan is usually located in the synagogue. Since parents have a duty of chinuch in regard to this obligation, just as they do for all other mitzvot, they should bring their children with them to services.

Chinuch for Daily Mitzvot 17

The poskim note that the purpose of bringing children to the synagogue is to teach them to stand with awe and reverence in the presence of God. It is therefore proper that children be taught to sit next to their parents, who supervise them to ensure that they read the prayers correctly. If, however, they are left to run about wildly, nothing is gained by bringing them. Since they disturb others it is better to leave them at home.[47] From this it also follows that toddlers and children too young to be controlled in the synagogue should not be brought to services at all. The mitzvah of chinuch is fulfilled only when children are taught proper respect for the sanctity of the synagogue. Furthermore there is reason for fear that allowing young children to engage in wild behavior during services will promote the opposite of chinuch. An attitude of disrespect for the sanctity of the synagogue may be instilled by doing this.[48]

What should parents do when both wish to attend services but they have a child who is not old enough? One solution is to use a hall or other room adjoining the synagogue proper (i.e., the sanctuary in which services take place) as a play area. At the times that they are allowed into the sanctuary, care must be taken that they are closely supervised and act properly.

Some synagogues attempt to hold children's interest in the prayers by sponsoring a junior congregation or youth service. Such activities are acceptable as long as parts of the service which require the presence of a minyan are not read. This means that the repetition of the Shemoneh Esreh and the Torah reading should be omitted unless ten males above the age of bar mitzvah are present.[49]

As just mentioned, a minor below the age of bar mitzvah cannot be counted towards the ten men needed for a minyan. There are, however, some opinions which allow the counting of a boy below the age of thirteen when there are nine adult males present and it is impossible to obtain a tenth. Others disagree.[50] Rabbi Yosef Caro rules according to the more restrictive opinion. He does not allow a boy below the age of thirteen to be counted towards a minyan under any circumstances. Rema, however, allows this in a case of great need.[51] *Magen Avraham* notes that the prevailing custom is to count a minor as the tenth when he holds a Chumash in his hands.[52] Many later authorities disagree with *Magen Avraham* and do not allow the counting of a minor even in a case of great necessity. Others, however, support the position.[53] Rabbi Moshe Feinstein allows one to rely on the lenient position of Rema and *Magen Avraham* when there is a possibility of the minyan dissolving as a result of the lack of a tenth man. He advises, however, that the boy hold a Torah scroll rather than a printed Chumash.[54]

The public reading of the Torah is one of the central parts of the synagogue service. The Torah is read on Mondays, Thursdays, Sabbaths, and holidays. On Shabbat, a minimum of seven people are called to the Torah, while on the other days fewer aliyot are called. The Talmud tells us that a minor boy can be included in the seven called to the Torah on Shabbat.[55] The *Shulchan Aruch* codifies this as halachah.[56] *Magen Avraham* points out that a minor can only be counted towards the seven people called on Shabbat, but not to the lesser number called on other days.[57] He further notes that the prevailing practice today is only to allow a minor to be called to Maftir, which is not an actual part of the required Torah reading. This is based on minority opinions which claim that the Talmud itself rules that a minor can be given the Maftir.[58] The later authorities all agree with this position.[59] However, it remains true that a minor can be called to say Maftir.[60] Some say that a minor should not be called to the Maftir of Shabbat Zachor or Shabbat Parah because these readings are the fulfillment of Torah requirements rather than rabbinic ordinances. The same is true for the Maftir of the first day of Shavuot, the seventh day of Pesach, and Shabbat Shuvah due to the special nature of these readings.[61] Obviously, a minor below the age of bar mitzvah who is called to chant Maftir must be mature enough to be able to read the words of the Haftorah correctly.[62]

There is one other honor connected with the Torah reading which it is customary to give to a boy below the age of bar mitzvah. When the actual reading of the Torah is completed, one person is given the honor of Hagbah, raising the Torah up, while another is called for Gelilah, the rolling and tying of the Torah scroll. The poskim state that nowadays it is customary to give the honor of Gelilah to minor boys in order to enable them to partake in the mitzvah of the Torah reading. As long as the boy involved is old enough to understand the holiness due to the Torah scroll, this is perfectly acceptable.[63] Likewise, we allow a minor to hold a second Torah scroll while the first one is being read from. This occurs on a day when more than one Torah reading is called for. Again, this is completely in order as long as the boy concerned is mature enough to understand what he is doing.[64]

Another important part of the synagogue service is Birchat Kohanim, the priestly blessing. Outside Israel the Ashkenazic practice is to reserve this blessing only for festivals. However, Ashkenazim in Israel and Sephardim throughout the world have this blessing as part of their daily Shachrit service.[65] The recitation of the priestly blessing by the Kohanim is a fulfillment of a positive biblical commandment. It would therefore seem that parents who are kohanim are required by the obligation of chinuch to train their sons to fulfill this mitzvah. The Mishnah however, rules that a minor should not take part in the Birchat Kohanim.[66] Rashi explains that it would violate the honor of the entire congregation to be blessed by a child. He concludes that under no circumstances should a minor participate in this mitzvah.[67] Tosafot disagrees and explains that the Mishnah forbids a minor to bless the congregation when he is the only kohen present but the minor is permitted to participate with other, adult kohanim. Indeed, the boy should do so, since he thereby fulfills the mitzvah of chinuch.[68] The *Shulchan Aruch* adopts the view of Tosafot.[69] The later authorities agree and specify that the boy should also be taught to make the blessing prior to the Birchat Kohanim as part of chinuch. They also state that the proper age for a minor to begin this practice is the point at which he is able to hold his hands in the proper position and utter the words of the blessings correctly.[70]

Blessings Before and After Food

The reciting of berachot, "blessings," prior to and after eating food is a requirement that applies to minors on the basis of chinuch. Since all adults, male and female, are obligated to observe these laws, both girls and boys must be educated to fulfill these requirements. The obligation of chinuch begins when the child is capable of understanding this law and fulfilling it.[71] It would seem that by the age of six or seven most children are in this category. Normally, it is considered to be a serious violation of Halachah to make a blessing using the full name of God just for demonstration purposes. A berachah in complete form should only be made when it is actually required. However, adults are permitted to make blessings using the full name of God when they do so in order to teach children how to say the berachot correctly. Even though the adult is not going to eat the particular food or perform the specific action, he may recite the full text of the berachah with the child as a fulfillment of the mitzvah of chinuch.[72]

Children must also be taught to recite the Birchat Hamazon, or Grace after Meals, as a fulfillment of chinuch.[73] This obligation also applies to both girls and boys, since women and men are equally obligated to say Birchat Hamazon.[74] Parents must begin teaching children to fulfill this mitzvah, just as they teach them to recite other berachot, from the age that the children are capable of understanding the mitzvah. There is, however, a special problem in that this group of berachot is too long to be learned in its entirety by young children, even if they are at an age where they understand the concept of thanking God for their food. In such cases, the parent must see to it that the child says some form of Grace after Meals. To solve this problem, *Magen Avraham* suggests that a shortened version of the first blessing of Birchat

Hamazon be taught to young children under the age of eight,⁷⁵ approximately. In the same way, such children should be taught an abbreviated form of the other blessings of this prayer. The version they use should gradually be increased until they learn the full text of the Birchat Hamazon.⁷⁶

The form of Birchat Hamazon used depends on whether one person is reciting this prayer or whether there are three or ten adult males present. In the latter two cases, a *zimun* exists and the grace is introduced in a special manner. Rabbi Yosef Caro, in the *Shulchan Aruch*, follows the opinion of Rishonim who allow a minor boy who is mature enough to understand the purpose and meaning of Birchat Hamazon to be counted towards the three or ten men needed for a *zimun*.⁷⁷ This can be as early as six for bright children, according to some opinions.⁷⁸ Rema, however, disagrees, stating that the correct practice is to not count a boy below the age of bar mitzvah towards *zimun*.⁷⁹ Ashkenazic practice today is in accordance with this opinion.⁸⁰ The later Sephardic authorities disagree and follow the opinion of Rabbi Yosef Caro.⁸¹

Notes

1. שו"ת מהרש"ל ע"ב, מגן אברהם ב' ס"ק ו'.
2. ט"ז ח' ס"ק ב'.
3. כף החיים ב', ט"ו.
4. האלף לך שלמה סימן ג', קיצור שולחן ערוך ג' סעיף ו'.
5. שו"ת אגרות משה או"ח ד' סימן ב', שערים המצויינים בהלכה ג' ס"ק ד'. It should be noted that by cases of necessity these *poskim* mean instances where a large financial loss would occur or cases of pressure by other equally unavoidable circumstances.
6. נדרים ל', עמוד ב'.
7. מגן אברהם ב' ס"ק ו'.
8. שולחן ערוך אורח חיים סימן ד'.
9. משנה ברורה ד', ס"ק י'.
10. פרי מגדים משבצות זהב ד' ס"ק ז', משנה ברורה שם ס"ק י'.
11. שולחן ערוך הרב סימן ד', סעיף ב'.
12. סוכה מ"ב, עמוד א'.

13. שולחן ערוך אורח חיים י״ז, סעיף ג׳.
14. מקור חיים החדש פרק כ״ח סעיף י״א, ליקוטי מהרי״ח סדר מצות ציצית.
15. ספר מהרי״ל, הלכות נישואין. Maharil bases this on the fact that the mitzvah of tzitzit is written in the Torah just before the mitzvah of marriage is referred to.
16. באר היטיב י״ז ס״ק ד׳, משנה ברורה שם ס״ק י׳.
17. ליקוטי מהרי״ח, סדר מצות ציצית.
18. מגן אברהם ח׳, ס״ק ג׳.
19. שערי תשובה י״ז ס״ק ד׳, ערוך השולחן או״ח, י״ז ס״ק ה׳.
20. כף החיים שם, ס״ק י׳.
21. שולחן ערוך אורח חיים ט״ז.
22. משנה ברורה י״ז, ס״ק ח׳.
23. שולחן ערוך אורח חיים מ׳.
24. סוכה מ״ב, עמוד א׳.
25. שולחן ערוך אורח חיים ל״ז, סעיף ג׳.
26. רמ״א שם.
27. מגן אברהם שם, ס״ק ד׳.
28. ב״ח שם.
29. ביאור הלכה שם, ד״ה וכן נהגו.
30. ערוך השולחן שם, סעיף ד׳.
31. חיי אדם כלל ס״ו סעיף ב׳, שערים המצויינים בהלכה י׳, ס״ק ל״ה.
32. שערים המצויינים בהלכה שם.
33. כף החיים ל״ז ס״ק י״ד, שו״ת יחוה דעת ח״ב סימן ד׳.
34. ברכות כ׳, עמוד א׳.
35. ביאור הלכה סימן ע׳ ד״ה קטנים.
36. שולחן ערוך אורח חיים סימן ע׳ סעיף ב׳.
37. כף החיים שם, ס״ק ו׳.
38. שולחן ערוך שם, סעיף א׳.
39. משנה ברורה שם, ס״ק ה׳.
40. משנה ברורה שם, ס״ק א׳.
41. שולחן ערוך אורח חיים ק״ו, סעיף א׳.
42. מגן אברהם שם, ס״ק ב׳.
43. משנה ברורה שם, ס״ק ב׳.
44. ערוך השולחן שם, ס״ק ז׳.
45. חידושי רעק״א סימן נ״ב, משנה ברורה סימן ע׳ ס״ק ב׳.
46. מגן אברהם ק״ו ס״ק ג׳, משנה ברורה שם ס״ק ה׳.
47. מגן אברהם קכ״ד ס״ק י״א, משנה ברורה צ״ח ס״ק ג׳.
48. מגן אברהם צ״ח ס״ק א׳, מחצית השקל שם, משנה ברורה שם ס״ק ג׳.
49. שו״ת אגרות משה ב׳ סימן צ״ח.
50. תוס׳ ד״ה ולית הלכתא, ברכות מ״ח עמוד א׳, בית יוסף סימן נ״ה.

Chinuch for Daily Mitzvot

51. שולחן ערוך אורח חיים נ"ה, סעיף ד'.
52. מגן אברהם שם, ס"ק ה'.
53. משנה ברורה שם, ס"ק כ"ד, שערים המצויינים בהלכה ט"ו, ס"ק א'.
54. שו"ת אגרות משה ב', סימן י"ח.
55. מגילה כ"ג, עמוד א'.
56. אורח חיים רפ"ב, סעיף ג'.
57. מגן אברהם שם, ס"ק ג', מחצית השקל שם.
58. מגן אברהם שם, ס"ק ו'.
59. משנה ברורה שם, ס"ק י"ב.
60. שולחן ערוך אורח חיים רפ"ד, סעיף ד'.
61. משנה ברורה רפ"ב, ס"ק כ"ג.
62. ביאור הלכה שם, ד"ה או בד' פרשיות.
63. משנה ברורה, סימן קמ"ז, ס"ק ז'.
64. שם, ס"ק כ"ט.
65. שולחן ערוך אורח חיים קכ"ט, סעיף א'.
66. מגילה כ"ד, עמוד א'.
67. רש"י שם, רש"י סוכה מ"ב, עמוד א' ד"ה חולקין לו.
68. תוס' ד"ה ואין, מגילה כ"ד, עמוד א'.
69. שולחן ערוך אורח חיים קכ"ח, סעיף ל"ד, בית יוסף שם.
70. משנה ברורה שם, ס"ק קכ"ג.
71. שולחן ערוך אורח חיים רט"ו, סעיף ג'.
72. שם, משנה ברורה שם, ס"ק י"ד.
73. שולחן ערוך אורח חיים קפ"ו, סעיף ב'.
74. שם, סעיף א'.
75. מגן אברהם קפ"ז, ס"ק א'.
76. משנה ברורה שם, ס"ק ד'.
77. שולחן ערוך אורח חיים קצ"ט, סעיף י'.
78. משנה ברורה שם, ס"ק כ"ד.
79. רמ"א שם, סעיף י'.
80. משנה ברורה שם, ס"ק כ"ז.
81. כף החיים שם, ס"ק ל"ד.

Chapter Three

Chinuch for Shabbat

There can be no doubt that the Sabbath is one of the most basic institutions ordained by the Torah, a sign of the covenant between God and the Jewish people. A violator of Shabbat is compared to an idolator who denies God.[1] The Talmud tells us that Shabbat is a precious gift which God took from His treasury and gave to the Jewish people.[2] It can easily be understood, therefore, that the mitzvah of chinuch applies with special emphasis to the observance of Shabbat. Perhaps to underline this fact, the *Shulchan Aruch* chooses the laws of Shabbat as the place most appropriate for a detailed discussion of the general requirements of chinuch as they apply to all mitzvot.[3] Shabbat has both positive and negative requirements. There are acts which the Jew must perform on the Sabbath and things which he is forbidden to do on that day. This chapter will discuss how children must be trained for both of these areas of Shabbat observance.

Preparations for Shabbat

The positive requirements of Shabbat begin before the day itself actually arrives. One should prepare for the coming of the Sabbath as if for the arrival of an honored guest. By doing this, one shows appreciation of the holiness of the day. The *Shulchan Aruch* states that it is a mitzvah to wash one's body and hair and cut one's nails in honor of Shabbat. In addition, if one's hair is long it should be cut.[4] Making such preparations for Shabbat may not be mandatory in the absolute sense, but it is certain that a mitzvah is performed when one does them.[5] This is true equally for both men and women.[6] Since this is so, parents are obligated to make sure that both boys and girls are prepared in this manner for the arrival of Shabbat. This requirement begins, as with other mitzvot, at the age when the child can understand that Shabbat is a special day which one needs to prepare for. It is recommended that these preparations take place on Friday so that it is obvious that they are being done in honor of Shabbat. However, if this is impossible they may be performed earlier.[7]

Besides these preparations, the *Shulchan Aruch* stresses that a person should change from his weekday clothes in honor of the beginning of Shabbat.[8] One should not wait until the morning of Shabbat to do this. Such behavior is considered demeaning to the Shabbat.[9] Women too should put on Shabbat clothing before lighting the candles.[10] As a result of the mitzvah of chinuch, parents are required to prepare their children, both boys and girls, in this manner for Shabbat. Again, the proper age to begin this preparation is when the child is old enough to understand that Shabbat is a special day. Often little children do not accompany their father to synagogue services on Friday night. When this occurs, parents should not think that it is unnecessary to dress them in their Sabbath finery. The *Chayei Adam* points out that a person should wear special clothes for Shabbat even when he is alone. Dressing in good clothing for Shabbat is done in honor of the day, not to impress the beholder.[11] Since this is so, the mitzvah of chinuch requires parents to ensure that their children put on their Shabbat clothing when Shabbat begins, whether or not anyone else will be seeing them.

Lighting of Candles

Lighting candles on Friday evening is one of the most beloved of the requirements of Shabbat. This mitzvah was instituted by the rabbis to promote peace and harmony in the home on the Sabbath.[12] Lighting candles is not a personal obligation. The individual Jew is not required to light Shabbat candles; rather each Jewish home must have lights burning in it on Shabbat.[13] Preference is given to women in lighting the candles. Only if there is no lady of the house, or if she is absent, should the male head of the household fulfill this mitzvah.[14]

Since the obligation of kindling Shabbat candles is not a personal requirement for the adult Jewish woman, it appears certain that parents do not have to see to it that their daughters perform this ceremony. Chinuch means educating the child for his or her future duties as an adult. If no such personal obligation exists for adults, there is no requirement of chinuch for children. Despite this, parents often express a desire for their daughters to light candles and bless them alongside their mother. Sometimes, little girls themselves request that they be allowed to do this. It may not be mandatory, according to Halachah, for girls to perform this mitzvah, but these families wish to have them do so voluntarily.

Some poskim express the opinion that such behavior is wrong. The act of a minor girl voluntarily lighting Shabbat candles cannot be faulted on halachic grounds. Nothing incorrect is done by this action. However, when the girl recites a berachah on the candles she performs the sin of making a *berachah she-einam tzerichah*, a halachically unnecessary blessing. Since no mitzvah is performed by the girl's lighting of the additional candles, no berachah may be made on them. This is true even if the girl's candles are lit in a different room than the mother's. According to these authorities, parents may allow their daughters to light Shabbat candles if they so wish. However, the daughters cannot be permitted to make the blessing over their candles under any circumstances.[15]

Other poskim disagree. The *Aruch HaShulchan* notes that the custom in his area was for daughters to light their own Shabbat candles with a berachah, despite the fact that they were still at home with their mother. He attempts to justify this practice by arguing that women have adopted this mitzvah as a personal obligation which pertains to each individual woman. Even though the lady of the house has lit her candles, a separate mitzvah is performed with each additional woman kindling her own lights. Since this is a questionable position, he recommends that the additional candles be lit with a berachah in different rooms of the house.[16] Other poskim concur with this argument. They note that, while it is difficult to justify halachically, there exits a widespread popular custom for women to consider the lighting of Shabbat candles as a personal obligation. It is because of this custom that a number of women sitting together for the Shabbat evening meal all light their own candles on the same table with a berachah, even though the lady of the house has already kindled her candles on the very same table.[17] If one follows the logic of this last position, it would be permissible for parents to allow their daughters to light Shabbat candles with a berachah alongside their mother.

Kiddush

The mitzvah of reciting Kiddush on Friday night is a personal Torah obligation incumbent on every Jew. This mitzvah has been rabbinically extended to require that the words of Kiddush be recited over a cup of wine, which is subsequently to be drunk.[18] The requirement to make Kiddush applies equally to both men and women.[19] Despite this fact, the popular custom is for the head of the household to make Kiddush for the female members of his family. They fulfill their requirement by listening to his Kiddush and having the intent that it relieve them of their obligation. They are only required to make their own Kiddush if they did not have this intent.[20]

The proper procedure for Kiddush in regard to male family members is subject to debate. There is no doubt that it is permissible for them to listen to the Kiddush made by the head of the family and thereby free themselves of their obligation, just as females do. The question remains, however, whether it is preferable for them to do so or to make their own individual Kiddush. Some poskim argue that the best course of action is for all males to make their own Kiddush.[21] Others disagree, preferring that one Kiddush be recited for the whole family.[22] The prevailing custom today is for each male in the family to recite his own individual Kiddush.[23]

The obligation of chinuch for children making Kiddush will depend on the preceding discussion. There is no doubt that a parent must have his minor sons and daughters fulfill the mitzvah of Kiddush. Since this is a personal obligation for all Jewish adults, children must be educated to fulfill it.[24] It is also clear that just as adults may fulfill their personal obligation of Kiddush by hearing this prayer recited by someone else so can children. The only question is whether it is appropriate for parents to encourage their children to make their own Kiddush rather than rely on the Kiddush made by an adult in their presence. It would appear that if one follows the opinion of the poskim that it is preferable for every individual to make Kiddush, then minor boys should be taught to say Kiddush on their own. Since as adults the best manner for them to perform this mitzvah will be by their own personal recitation of Kiddush, it is appropriate as a fulfillment of the obligation of chinuch to accustom them to this activity. Some Acharonim, however, argue that the duty of chinuch only pertains to the mandatory part of mitzvot and not to *hiddur mitzvah*, questions involving the best manner of performing a mitzvah versus the less preferred way.[25] Even these authorities agree that the point here is that parents are not required to accustom their minor boys to recite their own Kiddush. However, they may certainly teach them to do this if they so desire. In regard to girls it appears to be clear that there is no reason at all to educate them to say their own Kiddush. Since the prevailing custom, as mentioned earlier, is for adult women not to make Kiddush on their own but to hear it from another adult, there is certainly no obligation of chinuch to teach girls to do that which they will not perform as adult women.

A question often asked concerns the amount of wine a young boy must drink after making Kiddush. Normally an adult who makes Kiddush is required to drink a minimum amount known as *melo lugmav*, the equivalent of the amount of wine it would take to make that person's cheek bulge out if the wine was all concentrated on one side of his mouth. For the average person this is most of a *reve'it*, which will be defined below. For someone smaller than the average, it is debatable whether it is sufficient for him to drink the equivalent of *melo lugmav*, or whether he is required to drink most of a standard *reve'it* regardless of the size of his mouth. Despite this, all opinions agree that a minor who makes Kiddush to fulfill the mitzvah of chinuch is not obligated to drink more than his own *melo lugmav*. This would mean that each child would be required to drink the amount of wine appropriate to the size of his mouth.[26]

It should be noted that this discussion does not concern the appropriate size for the Kiddush cup. Kiddush must always be made on a full *reve'it* of wine, no matter how much of that wine will subsequently be drunk.[27] This is true even when a minor makes Kiddush to fulfill the mitzvah of chinuch.[28] The size of a *reve'it* is subject to debate. According to the opinion of Rabbi Moshe Feinstein, this amount is, at a minimum, the equivalent of 3.3 ounces.[29] This would mean that parents who want their sons to make Kiddush as a fulfillment of the mitzvah of chinuch should make sure that the cup used holds at least this amount of wine.[30] It is, unfortunately, common for smaller cups to be used for children's Kiddush.

Frequently mothers who are widowed or divorced request that their minor sons make Kiddush for the entire family in place of their father. This procedure is unacceptable. Even though children are required to make Kiddush, their obligation is only rabbinic in origin since it results from the mitzvah of chinuch. Adults, on the other hand, whether male or female, are required to make Kiddush as a Torah obligation. A boy below the age of adulthood cannot free an adult of a Torah obligation, because there is no such stringent requirement on the minor.[31] Since this involves a question of Torah law we do not consider the boy an adult here merely because he has reached the age of thirteen. Physical evidence of maturity is required, as indicated by a beard sprouting over most of his face. Until that point is reached, the adult women of the house should make Kiddush for themselves. If they do not know the requisite amount of Hebrew to do this, they should repeat the Kiddush after the boy word for word. By doing this they fulfill their personal obligation of Kiddush.[32]

Shabbat Meals

A Jew is obligated to eat three meals during the course of Shabbat. This requirement applies to both men and women.[33] Each of these meals must begin with *lechem mishneh*, two whole loaves of bread on which the blessing of Hamotzi is recited. This obligation also applies equally to both men and women, according to most opinions.[34] The normal procedure is for the head of the household to make the blessing over the two loaves of bread, and have the intent thereby to free all present from the obligation of *lechem mishneh*. Everyone present then either says "Amen" to this blessing or makes his own blessing on his individual piece of bread. Different customs exist as to which of these procedures is preferable. However, it is certain that either way one fulfills his obligation in regard to this law.[35] Since these laws apply to both male and female adults, it is obvious that they apply to children of both sexes on the basis of the mitzvah of chinuch. Parents are required to accustom their children to fulfill these obligations from the age at which they are mature enough to understand their meaning.

Besides the Friday night Kiddush, the noontime meal of Shabbat is preceded by the recitation of a different Kiddush. The saying of this Kiddush is a rabbinic obligation rather than a Torah one.[36] It is clear that the mitzvah of chinuch requires parents to see to it that their children hear the recitation of this second Kiddush.

There is an important difference between adults and children. Adults are not permitted to eat or drink before reciting the Kiddush. On Friday night this prohibition begins with the onset of

Shabbat,[37] while on Shabbat morning it comes into force after the conclusion of Shachrit.[38] Even though children are obligated to hear Kiddush at these two times in the same way as adults are, they are not restricted from eating prior to the recitation of Kiddush.

There are a number of reasons for this. First, the requirement of chinuch does not prohibit giving children something which they need for their health, such as food, at specific times of the day or year. In addition, there are opinions that even adults may eat before Kiddush. While we do not accept this in regard to adults, we rely on it for the needs of children. Because of this, children are permitted to drink from the wine used for Kiddush in the synagogue on Friday night. Otherwise doing so would be forbidden, since the children would be drinking before hearing the mandatory Kiddush which comes together with their Friday night meal. It is forbidden to be stringent about this and restrict children who want to eat or drink prior to Kiddush from doing so.[39]

Havdalah

The end of Shabbat is commemorated with the Havdalah ceremony. The obligation to make Havdalah, or to hear it made, applies to all Jewish males. There is a disagreement, however, among the Rishonim as to whether women are also required to make Havdalah. Rabbi Yosef Caro rules in accord with the opinion that women are obligated.[40] Rema disagrees. He states that we should take the opinion that women are exempt from Havdalah into consideration. This means that we have to consider the question unresolved. Since we do not know whether women are or are not obligated to make Havdalah, women should not make Havdalah on their own but rather be sure to hear it from men. If they were to make Havdalah on their own, and in fact they are exempt from this requirement, they would be making an unnecessary blessing. However, when a woman hears Havdalah made by a man she certainly fulfills her own obligation, if indeed such an obligation does exist.[41] *Magen Avraham* and many other Acharonim disagree with Rema, maintaining that there is nothing objectionable about women making Havdalah on their own.[42]

All these opinions agree that in the final analysis women are required to hear Havdalah just as men are. The only question is whether or not women should make it themselves. Since this is so, there is no doubt that the mitzvah of chinuch requires parents to make sure that their children, both boys and girls, hear Havdalah at the end of Shabbat. As with other mitzvot, this obligation begins from the age at which the individual child is mature enough to understand this particular requirement.

One distinction which separates Havdalah from Kiddush is the manner in which one distributes the wine over which the berachah has been made. At Kiddush everyone present is given some of the wine to drink. *Magen Avraham* states that it is not proper for women to drink from the wine of Havdalah.[43] This means that girls should not be given a portion from the Havdalah cup. However. *Magen Avraham* notes that it is proper for the person making Havdalah to drink the entire cup of wine himself and not give anyone a portion of it.[44] In keeping with this practice, boys should also not receive any of the Havdalah wine. These restrictions are not universally accepted. Some opinions encourage giving the Havdalah wine to male family members.[45] The *Aruch HaShulchan* notes that the restriction on women is not accepted by all and that many women do drink from the Havdalah cup.[46] The *Mishnah Brurah*, on the other hand, regards the custom of not giving Havdalah wine to women as binding.[47] Other opinions seem to support the position of the *Aruch HaShulchan*.[48]

A widowed or divorced mother should not ask her minor son to recite Havdalah for the entire family. She should make Havdalah herself. The logic for this is exactly the same as it is for Kiddush. Children are only required to recite or to hear Kiddush by rabbinic law, while adults are so mandated by Torah law. This is true for females as well as males according to the majority of poskim. A boy below the age of thirteen cannot free an adult of a Torah obligation, since no such requirement is incumbent on a minor.[49] Again, as with Kiddush, we do not consider a boy an adult here merely because he has reached the age of bar mitzvah. Instead, we require physical evidence of maturity, which is indicated by a beard sprouting over most of the face. This is true because we are dealing with a question of Torah law rather than rabbinic requirements. Until that point is reached the mother should recite Havdalah herself. If necessary, she may repeat the Hebrew of Havdalah after her son word for word. When she does this she fulfills her personal Torah requirement.[50]

Forbidden Labor and Children

Parents are required to stop children from performing halachically forbidden acts, as discussed in the first chapter of this work. This duty is part of the obligation of chinuch. In keeping with this principle, parents are obligated to train their children not to violate Shabbat by performing any act of prohibited labor on that day. This means that from the age at which the child possesses the maturity to understand that a particular action is forbidden on Shabbat, parents must stop him or her from doing such an action. This age will differ from child to child.[51] This is true when the child initiates such an action on his own. Even before the child reaches the age of understanding it is forbidden for the parent to actively cause a child to violate Shabbat. This prohibition begins at birth.[52]

It is clear that children, even at a very young age, may not be used to violate Shabbat prohibitions for the benefit of their parents. For example, if an electric switch is left off or on and the parent wants it to be moved to the opposite position he may not tell the child to perform this task. In such a case, the parent would be actively causing the child to sin by telling him to violate Shabbat. This is true for any child, no matter how young he or she may be. Even in cases where one is allowed to ask a non-Jew to do forbidden work on Shabbat for the benefit of a Jew, it is not permissible to do so with a child. If a non-Jew is not present, a Jewish child may not be substituted for him.[53]

Turei Zahav argues that a parent can directly tell a child to do an action which violates Shabbat when the action is only rabbinically prohibited.[54] Later Acharonim say that even according to *Turei Zahav* this is only permitted when the violation of Shabbat is done for the sake of a mitzvah.[55] However, the majority of authorities do not allow a Shabbat violation by a child even for this purpose.[56] The only time they see a possibility for allowing an adult to actively cause a child to do a rabbinically forbidden act on Shabbat is when the child does this action to satisfy his own needs. There are poskim who permit this in such a case. Needless to say, according to these authorities, the parent does not have to stop a child, even from the age of chinuch and onwards, from performing such an action on his own.[57] The *Shulchan Aruch* does not accept this as permitted, but many Acharonim do. The essential element for allowing this is the fact that the action is being done for the child's benefit rather than for the parent's.[58]

Carrying on Shabbat

One of the prohibitions of Shabbat is carrying from the private domain into the public domain or vice versa. In addition, one is forbidden to carry more than four *amot*, or cubits, in the public domain itself. There is no doubt that the mitzvah of chinuch applies to this prohibition, as it does to all Shabbat requirements. Parents are required to stop their children from carrying on Shabbat from the time at which the child is mature enough to understand that such action is forbidden on that day. Even before that age, parents may not cause their children to carry by giving them objects or by telling them to perform this act. The opinion, mentioned earlier, which permits parents to cause a child to sin when it is for the benefit of the child, will similarly allow a parent to give the child things to carry when such objects are necessary for the benefit of the child.

A question which frequently arises is whether parents may give a child their house key to carry on Shabbat. It would seem that this should be forbidden, since the parent is instructing the child to violate the Shabbat. However, *Turei Zahav* claims that this is permitted, since according to most poskim our public domain is not a *reshut harabbim*, and it is only rabbinically forbidden to carry there.[59] The overwhelming majority of poskim reject this argument. They state that a parent may not cause his child, or even allow his child, to carry on Shabbat even if carrying is only a rabbinic violation of Shabbat.[60]

Many of the authorities who dispute the opinion of *Turei Zahav* allow a child to be given an object, such as a siddur, to carry to the synagogue on Shabbat, when the child will subsequently use the siddur himself. In this case, the child is permitted to commit a rabbinic violation of Shabbat for his own benefit. This is forbidden under any other circumstances.[61] Others do not even allow the child to carry objects such as a siddur for his own use. According to them, only in cases of extreme need can one permit such a violation of Shabbat by a child.[62] It is clear that according to both these opinions a father is not permitted to give his child a talit to carry to the synagogue on Shabbat for the father's later use.

It is common for a child who goes for a walk on Shabbat with his parents to pick up objects in the street which stimulate his interest. Parents often ask if they must stop the child from carrying such items. The answer to this question depends on the age of the child. If the minor is below the age at which he is capable of understanding that it is wrong to carry, then parents do not have to stop him from doing this. If, however, the child is past this point, the parents are required by the mitzvah of chinuch to stop their child from violating Shabbat. This is true even though the child is picking up these objects for his own usage and benefit. Most of the authorities who allow a child to carry for his own benefit only do so in cases of great need or for the purpose of a mitzvah. These conditions obviously do not apply in this case.[63].

Games and Toys

The obligation of training a child to refrain from forbidden labor on Shabbat raises the most problems in regard to games and toys. Many of them are prohibited for Shabbat use for various reasons. Parents are consequently faced with the question of whether they may or may not permit their children to play with such objects on Shabbat. It should be noted that the entire discussion here concerns boys and girls below the age of bar or bat mitzvah. Children above that age are considered adults. The poskim strongly advise adults to refrain from playing games on Shabbat even when such activities do not technically violate Shabbat.[64]

Toys which produce music or make noise while one plays with them are considered to be *muktzeh*. This is because the primary purpose of such toys is to make noise, which is a prohibited activity on Shabbat.[65] Since this is so, it is forbidden to play with them, or even move them, on Shabbat. Despite this, parents do not have to stop a child from playing with such toys if the child is too young to understand that they are forbidden on Shabbat. This is because there is no obligation of chinuch for a child so young. However, it would appear that the parent cannot bring such a toy to the child or move the toy himself. If he did so, he would be directly causing the child to sin. Furthermore, if the child is at an age where he can understand that such a toy is forbidden on Shabbat, it would be incumbent on the parents to stop him from playing with this object. Some authorities argue that parents are permitted to give toys of this kind to children to play with. They base their position on the views of those who allow parents to cause a child to violate a rabbinic prohibition of Shabbat when this is done for the benefit of the child.[66] Others disagree.[67]

Stones and sticks are other objects which are *muktzeh*. Small children often want to play with these items. Here again, permis-

Chinuch for Shabbat

sibility depends on the maturity of the child. If, however, the stones or sticks were designated to be used permanently by the child as toys before the beginning of Shabbat, they are no longer *muktzeh* and may be moved by anyone, even an adult.[68]

Playing in a sandbox is a popular pastime for small children. If the sand has been designated for use as a plaything prior to Shabbat, there is no probem of *muktzeh* in playing with it.[69] Even children who have reached the age of understanding are permitted to engage in this activity. This holds if the sand is so fine that when some of it is removed no hole is created because the surrounding sand immediately fills the depression created. If this is not the case, a violation of Shabbat is involved, since it is prohibited to dig a hole on Shabbat.[70] In such a case, parents must stop children above the age of understanding from engaging in this activity. While children may play in fine sand, they may not pour water on it and mix the water with the sand. This activity constitutes a violation of Shabbat, since kneading of the sand and water occurs.[71] Here again, parents do not have to restrain toddlers below the age of understanding from performing such an activity. An additional problem exists with regard to covering the sandbox. Unless the cover to the box is on hinges, the adult who removes or replaces the cover violates Shabbat by creating or destroying an *ohel*, or roof. In such a case, the sandbox would have to be left open from before Shabbat.[72]

Balls are not *muktzeh*. There is no problem in allowing children of any age to play with them on Shabbat.[73] Of course, if the ball is thrown or carried in the public domain, without an *eruv*, the prohibition of carrying will be violated. However, when the ball is played with inside a house or in an enclosed area, there is no such problem. Even in an enclosed yard or within an *eruv*, children should not be allowed to play games like soccer, which involve rolling or kicking a ball on the ground. This is due to the rabbinic prohibition of rolling objects on the ground, since such objects tend to make holes or fill holes in the earth.[74] Included in this category are the large balls which toddlers roll and kick on the ground. When such games are played inside the house on the floor they are permissible. This is because contemporary houses do not have earthen floors. Out of doors, however, it is forbidden to play in this manner even on a concrete or stone floor or patio. Since the majority of yards are not paved, the rabbinic prohibition applies to all outdoor areas without distinction.[75] These distinctions apply to playing with marbles on the floor in exactly the same way as they do to playing with balls. Here, again, parents are not required to stop young children below the age of understanding from engaging in such activities on their own. They cannot, however, encourage their child to play in this manner or participate with him in such a game. It should be added that inflatable balls, such as beachballs, which are blown up and then tied are considered *muktzeh*. If, however, they are merely inflated but not tied they are not *muktzeh* and may be moved by anyone.[76]

A bicycle is considered to be *muktzeh* since its primary purpose is to carry its rider through the public domain on Shabbat. Therefore, it may not be ridden by a child even inside the house or in an enclosed yard.[77] This is not true of a tricycle. Tricycles are not *muktzeh*, and children of any age can be permitted to ride them inside the house or within an *eruv*. Of course, they may not do so outside the *eruv*, since this would constitute carrying on Shabbat.[78]

Many toys made for young children operate by means of a spring. When the spring is wound up the toy operates for a set period of time. Some authorities say that winding up such a toy is a violation of Shabbat. Since this is so, neither adults nor children who have reached the age of understanding may wind such a toy.[79] Again, parents would not have to stop children below this age from doing this. Other authorities regard this activity as permissible even for older children and parents.[80]

Building blocks and beads of various kinds are also popular toys. When the blocks do not interlock with one another there is no problem in allowing children to play with them. Even when the various pieces do interlock with one another it is permissible for children to connect them, as long as they merely fit together and are not joined by screws or knocked together with force. When, however, the pieces are tightly joined together by screws or other means, it constitutes a violation of Shabbat to fit them together. In such a case, parents are required to stop children who have reached the age of understanding from playing with these toys.[81]

There is generally no problem with allowing older children to play board games, such as chess or checkers.[82] However, playing such games is forbidden when it is the normal practice for players to keep score by writing. This is prohibited by rabbinic decree even though in this particular case the players will not record their score.[83] Parents are required to stop their children from engaging in such games. It is also questionable as to whether playing a game like Monopoly, which uses play money, is permissible on Shabbat. There are, however, authorities who consider this to be completely permissible.[84] If one follows this opinion, parents do not have to restrict their children from such games on Shabbat.

Games like Scrabble, which involve placing letters next to one another, are a special case. There is no problem with putting the letters next to one another as long as they are not placed in a surrounding frame which fixes them in a position attached to one another. When a player puts them in an attached position, he performs the forbidden act of writing on Shabbat. However, as long as this does not occur, there is no violation of Shabbat.[85] If it is the practice for players to keep score during such games, however, it is forbidden to play with them on Shabbat. Jigsaw puzzles are also forbidden on Shabbat. Since the pieces of these puzzles fit tightly together and become one attached piece, it is forbidden to assemble them on Shabbat. When a person does so he violates the prohibition of writing, which includes drawing a picture.[86] Parents are obligated to teach their children not to assemble puzzles on Shabbat.

Children are permitted to play games which involve running and jumping on Shabbat. Since such activities are pleasurable for children, they are not considered inappropriate to the spirit of the day.[87] It is, however, rabbinically forbidden to climb or even lean against trees on Shabbat.[88] Similarly, one is not allowed to climb a ladder leaning against a tree.[89] Parents are therefore obligated to stop children who wish to play games involving such activities from doing so. This is part of the parental duty of chinuch for the negative mitzvot of Shabbat. Again, parents are not required to stop children below the age of understanding from leaning against or playing with trees or plants on Shabbat.

It is prohibited for an adult to blow bubbles with a bubble pipe on Shabbat or Yom Tov. By doing this, a person violates the sanctity of these days, since he creates new forms out of the soap solution when he blows the bubbles. It is however, not necessary for a parent to stop a child, even *above* the age of understanding, from engaging in such activities on these days.[90]

The blowing up of air balloons is permitted on Shabbat or Yom Tov under certain conditions. If the balloon is not tied or knotted after it is filled with air, but merely closed by a stopper which fits into a preexisting opening in the balloon, there is no restriction on blowing it up on these days. This is true even if the balloon has the shape of an animal or some other object after it is filled. However, if the balloon must be tied after being filled with air, it may not be blown up on these days.[91] It is always forbidden to make snowballs or a snowman on Shabbat. This constitutes building, since the snow particles are firmly put together to form a new structure. Parents are required to stop children above the age of understanding from engaging in such activities on Shabbat. It is, however, permissible for children to touch snow on Shabbat even if the snow fell on the same day. Snow is not considered to be *muktzeh*.[92]

Notes

1. חולין דף ה׳, עמוד א׳, רש״י ד״ה "אלא לאו" שם.
2. ביצה דף ט״ז, עמוד א׳.
3. אורח חיים, סימן שמ״ג.
4. אורח חיים סימן ר״ס, סעיף א׳.
5. דרכי משה ר״ס ס״ק א׳, משנה ברורה שם ס״ק א׳.
6. משנה ברורה שם ס״ק ב׳.
7. ט״ז ר״ס ס״ק א׳, מגן אברהם ריש סימן ר״ס.
8. אורח חיים סימן רס״ב, סעיף ב׳.
9. ברכי יוסף רס״ב, ס״ק ד׳.
10. משנה ברורה רס״ב, ס״ק י״א.
11. חיי אדם הלכות שבת, כלל ה׳ ס״ק ז׳.
12. תוספות ד״ה "הדלקת נר" שבת דף כ״ה, עמוד ב׳.
13. אורח חיים סימן רס״ג, סעיף ב׳.
14. שם, סעיף ג׳, משנה ברורה שם ס״ק י״א.
15. שו״ת יחוה דעת, ח״ב סימן ל״ב, ספר חובת הדר, פרק מצות הדלקת נר שבת ס״ק כ״ח.
16. ערוך השולחן רס״ג, סעיף ז׳.
17. מנחת שבת, סימן ע״ה, ס״ק ל״א.
18. משנה תורה, הלכות שבת, פרק כ״ט הלכות א׳-ו׳, משנה ברורה רע״א ס״ק ב׳.
19. אורח חיים סימן רע״א, סעיף ב׳.
20. מגן אברהם קצ״ג, ס״ק ב׳. *Magen Avraham* recommends that the women say the words of Kiddush quietly together with the head of the household. Other authorities disagree. See שערי תשובה, סימן רצ״ו, ס״ק ג׳
21. אליה רבה סימן רע״ג, ס״ק ט׳.
22. הגהות הגאון מברעזאן, מובא בספר ליקוטי מהרי״ח סדר קידוש דליל שבת.
23. ספר ליקוטי מהרי״ח סדר קידוש דליל שבת.
24. משנה ברורה סימן רע״א, ס״ק ב׳.
25. ביאור הלכה סימן תרע״ה סעיף ג׳, ד״ה "ולדידן".
26. ביאור הלכה סימן רע״א, סעיף י״ג, ד״ה "והוא רובו".
27. מגן אברהם סימן רע״א ס״ק כ״ד, משנה ברורה שם, ס״ק נ״א.
28. חק יעקב סימן תע״ב, ס״ק כ״ז, פמ״ג אשל אברהם שם, ס״ק י״ז.
29. הגדה קול דודי, סימן ב׳, ס״ק ו׳.
30. The Chafetz Chaim advises that for Friday night Kiddush it is appropriate to use a cup that holds an even more stringent amount of wine. See ביאור הלכה סימן רע״א, סעיף י״ג, ד״ה "של רביעית".
31. מגן אברהם סימן רע״א, ס״ק ב׳, משנה ברורה שם, ס״ק ג׳.
32. משנה ברורה שם. It should be noted that in a case where the women have already said the Friday night Shemoneh Esreh it is acceptable for a minor boy to

make Kiddush for them. See שו"ת רבי עקיבא איגר, סימן ז', ביאור הלכה סימן רע"א, סעיף א', ד"ה „מיד" בסופו.
33. חיי אדם הלכות שבת, כלל ז', ס"ק א'.
34. פמ"ג משבצות זהב, סימן רע"ד, ס"ק א', משנה ברורה שם ס"ק א'. See שאלות ותשובות האלף לך שלמה סימן קי"ד who argues that women are exempt from this obligation.
35. שו"ת מלמד להועיל, חלק א', סימן כ"ד.
36. משנה ברורה סימן רפ"ט, ס"ק ג'.
37. אורח חיים סימן רע"א, סעיף ד'.
38. מגן אברהם, סימן רפ"ו, ס"ק א', משנה ברורה שם, ס"ק ז'.
39. מגן אברהם, סימן רס"ט, ס"ק א', משנה ברורה שם, ס"ק א'.
40. אורח חיים סימן רצ"ו, סעיף ח', שו"ת יחוה דעת, חלק ד', סימן כ"ז.
41. רמ"א שם.
42. מגן אברהם שם, ס"ק י"א, משנה ברורה שם, ס"ק ל"ה.
43. מגן אברהם שם, ס"ק ד'.
44. מגן אברהם שם.
45. אליה רבה שם, ס"ק ד'.
46. ערוך השולחן שם, סעיף ה'.
47. משנה ברורה שם, ס"ק ד'.
48. חיי אדם הלכות שבת, כלל ח', ס"ק י"ב, עיין מקור חיים השלם, פרק קל"ח, ס"ק כ"ד.
49. מגן אברהם, סימן רע"א, ס"ק ב', משנה ברורה שם, ס"ק ג'.
50. משנה ברורה שם.
51. חיי אדם כלל ס"ו, ס"ק ג', משנה ברורה סימן שמ"ג, ס"ק ג'.
52. חיי אדם שם ס"ק ו', משנה ברורה שם ס"ק ג'.
53. שו"ת חתם סופר, חלק ו', סימן י"ג.
54. ט"ז סימן שמ"ו, ס"ק ו'.
55. פמ"ג משבצות זהב שם, שו"ת חתם סופר, חלק ו', סימן י"ג.
56. מנחת שבת פ"ב, ס"ק ב', שערים המצויינים בהלכה, פ"ב, ס"ק ב'.
57. שו"ת רשב"א, ח"א, סימן צ"ב, פירוש הר"ן בתחילת מסכת יומא.
58. אורח חיים סימן שמ"ג, ביאור הלכה שם ד"ה „מד"ס", שערים המצויינים בהלכה, פ"ב, ס"ק ב'.
59. ט"ז סימן שמ"ו, ס"ק ו'.
60. מנחת שבת פ"ב, ס"ק ב', שערים המצויינים בהלכה, פ"ב, ס"ק ב'.
61. שו"ת רעק"א סימן ט"ו, שו"ת חתם סופר ח"ו סימן י"ג, ביאור הלכה סימן שמ"ג ד"ה „מד"ס. It must be noted that these authorities permitted this in their time, when siddurim were not commonly available in synagogues.
62. חיי אדם כלל ס"ו, סעיף ו'.
62a. חכמת אדם, כלל קנ"ב, סעיף י"ז.
63. חיי אדם שם. שו"ת מהר"ם שי"ק או"ח, סימן קע"ג. It also must be remembered that the *Shulchan Aruch* itself does not accept the lenient opinion which allows children to violate Shabbat rabbinically when they do it for their own benefit.

64. משנה ברורה סימן של"ז, ס"ק כ"א, כף החיים סימן ש"ח, ס"ק רנ"ט.
65. פמ"ג אשל אברהם של"ח, ס"ק ג'.
66. שמירת שבת כהלכתה, פרק ט"ז, סעיף ג'.
67. הטיפול בתינוק בשבת ויום טוב, פרק י"ג, סעיף א'. Also see the opinions cited earlier in n. 63.
68. אורח חיים סימן ש"ח, סעיף כ"ב.
69. אורח חיים שם, סעיף ל"ח.
70. משנה ברורה שם, ס"ק קמ"ג.
71. משנה ברורה סימן שכ"א, ס"ק ו'.
72. אורח חיים סימן שט"ו, סעיף ב', משנה ברורה שם, ס"ק י"ז.
73. אורח חיים סימן ש"ח, סעיף מ"ה, משנה ברורה שם, ס"ק קנ"ח.
74. משנה ברורה שם.
75. ביאור הלכה סימן של"ז, סעיף ב', ד"ה „ויש".
76. שמירת שבת כהלכתה, פרק ט"ז, סעיף ח'.
77. דעת הגר"מ פיינשטיין הובא בספר טלטולי שבת מאת הרב באדנער, פרק א', הערה כ"א, שמירת שבת כהלכתה, פרק ט"ז, סעיף י"ז. Rabbi Yosef Chaim of Baghdad permits the riding of a bicycle within an *eruv* even by adults. This opinion, however, is not generally accepted. See כף החיים, סימן ת"ד, ס"ק ח'.
78. דעת הגר"מ פיינשטיין הובא בספר טלטולי שבת, פרק א', הערה כ"ב, שמירת שבת כהלכתה, פרק ט"ז, סעיף י"ז.
79. דעת הגר"מ פיינשטיין הובא בספר טלטולי שבת, פרק א', הערה ל"ו.
80. דעת הגרש"ז אויערבאך, שמירת שבת כהלכתה, פרק ט"ז, סעיף י"ד.
81. אורח חיים סימן שי"ד סעיף א', סימן שי"ג, סעיף ו', שמירת שבת כהלכתה, פרק ט"ז, סעיף י"ח.
82. אורח חיים סימן של"ח, סעיף ה'.
83. חיי אדם, הלכות שבת, כלל ל"ח, סעיף י"א.
84. שמירת שבת כהלכתה, פרק ט"ז, סעיף ל"ב, שם הערה פ"ד.
85. חיי אדם הלכות שבת, כלל ל"ז, נשמת אדם ס"ק ב', שו"ת אגרות משה או"ח חלק א', סימן קל"ה.
86. משנה תורה, הלכות שבת, פרק י"א, הלכה י"ז, משנה ברורה סימן ש"מ, ס"ק כ"ב.
87. אורח חיים סימן ש"א, סעיף ב', משנה ברורה שם, ס"ק ה'
88. אורח חיים סימן של"ו, סעיף א'.
89. שם, סעיף י"ג.
90. שמירת שבת כהלכתה, פרק ט"ז, סעיף ל'.
91. שם, סעיף ח'.
92. שם, סעיף מ"ד.

Chapter Four

Chinuch for Festivals

The different holidays of the year are the highpoints of the Jewish calendar. Each of the festivals brings its own special mitzvot and prohibitions. By fulfilling these religious requirements Jews are enabled to link themselves anew to their heritage and their history. The festivals have both positive and negative duties, just as the Sabbath does. The obligation of chinuch applies to these requirements in the same way as it does to all other mitzvot of the Torah. This chapter will give a review of the mitzvah of chinuch as it pertains to all the special occasions of the Jewish year.

Passover and Chametz Medication

The prohibitions of the holiday of Pesach center on the subject of chametz. A Jew is forbidden to eat chametz, benefit from chametz, or even own chametz throughout the festival. These prohibitions are Torah ordinances which apply to all Jews, both male and female.[1] Since this is so, it is clear that the duty of chinuch for both boys and girls applies to these mitzvot, just as it does to all other laws. Parents are required to stop their children from eating chametz or benefiting from chametz from the age at which the child can understand that such an action is wrong. Below that age parents are not obligated to stop children from such activities. Despite this, however, they may not give chametz to a child from birth onwards, just as they may not cause a child to sin in any other way.

The laws of chametz usually cause few problems. However, when a sick child requires a chametz medication, whether for internal or external use, other rules apply. Obviously, if the illness is life-threatening, there is no restriction on using any means to cure it. When the sickness is serious but not life-threatening, things are more complicated. *Magen Avraham* states that in such a case the parent should ask a non-Jew to carry the child into a non-Jewish house and there administer the medication.[2] The rationale here is that telling a non-Jew to violate a Torah prohibition for the benefit of a Jew is only rabbinically forbidden. The rabbis did not forbid this in a case of illness, even when the sickness is not life-threatening. If, however, the parent himself administered the medication he, as a Jew, would be personally violating a Torah prohibition. Such a violation can only be permitted in a case of danger to life.[3] All efforts should be made to have the chametz given to the child outside of the parents' home. This is because of the Torah prohibition on a Jew having chametz in his possession on Pesach.

If it is impossible to move the child, it is permissible to have the non-Jew bring his own chametz into the Jewish home and give it to him. The non-Jew should remove the chametz medication from the house when he finishes administering it to the child and bring it back with him when it is needed again. If this is also impossible, the medication can be left in the Jew's house for the necessary period of treatment, as long as the non-Jew remains the owner of the chametz medication. However, the parent is never allowed to administer the medication. Each time it is needed this must be done by a non-Jew or a minor.[4] The Jewish parent, in such a case, must make sure that he does not become the halachic owner of the chametz medication left in his home. He establishes this by verbally declaring at the time the non-Jew brings it into his house that he does not want to obtain ownership of it. The parent must be careful under all circumstances not to give the non-Jew money in advance to buy the medication. If he does this, he becomes the halachic owner of the chametz.[5]

There is a dispute among the poskim as to the correct course of action when the non-Jew refuses to buy the medication without payment. *Magen Avraham* states that in such a case the parent is allowed to promise the non-Jew that he will reimburse him for his expenses after the purchase. This is permitted because it is considered to be paying back a debt rather than purchasing chametz.[6] Other authorities prohibit this. They argue that when the Jew makes such an arrangement he is considered to be buying chametz on Pesach.[7] Most later authorities agree with *Magen Avraham*. If the non-Jew demands payment, the parent may promise to reimburse him after the purchase.[8] It is apparently not permissible to give the non-Jew the money in advance, even if he insists on this arrangement in order to purchase the medicine. *Aruch HaShulchan*, however, notes that this is permitted if even a small doubt exists that the untreated illness might develop into a life-threatening condition.[9] When the chametz medication is left in the Jew's home over Pesach it should be locked away with the ordinary chametz which was sold before the holiday. If this is not possible, then it should be separated from the rest of the house by a barrier with the height of ten tefachim or at least be completely covered up when not in use.[10]

Food for Babies on Pesach

A different problem exists with foods used to feed babies. It is clear that baby cereals and foods which contain chametz cannot be used on Pesach. Parents are forbidden to give infants prohibited food from the time of their birth.[11] Since chametz on Pesach is certainly included in this category, substitutes for chametz foods must be found.

A common question concerns infant formula. These liquids are the sole source of nourishment for infants who are not breast-feeding during their first months of life. Medical opinion considers cow's milk an inadequate substitute for formula. Babies should not be given cow's milk before reaching a certain point in their development. Parents with children on formula are therefore faced with a serious problem in feeding them over Pesach.

The solution to this problem is found in the fact that baby formula does not contain real chametz substances. Chametz is defined by Halachah as the product of wheat, barley, oats, rye, or spelt mixed with water and allowed to ferment. Any other grain or grainlike substance does not become chametz and is permitted on Pesach.[12] Despite this, Ashkenazic communities have accepted as a binding restriction on themselves that all such foods, known as *kitniyot*, are also to be regarded as chametz and not to be eaten on Passover. These substances, even according to Ashkenazic practice, are only forbidden to be eaten. There is no restriction on benefiting from their use or owning them on Pesach.[13]

The chametz contained in baby formula is exclusively of the *kitniyot* variety, and there is no problem about keeping such substances in one's possession during Pesach. Moreover, though it might seem that Ashkenazic parents should not be allowed to feed formula to infants on the holiday, this is not so. The prohibition of *kitniyot*, is suspended whenever there is a lack of alternative food sources and hunger would result,[14] and this rule certainly applies in this case. There is no restriction on feeding *kitniyot* to infants, but the formula should be prepared and served on separate dishes and utensils. Furthermore, once a baby can be changed to cow's milk without any adverse reaction, there is no justification for continuing to use formula on Pesach.

After infants are introduced to solid food, baby cereal generally becomes a staple in their diet. These foods are, of course, real chametz rather than *kitniyot*, and cannot be fed to babies on Pesach. Many children will not accept ordinary matzah as a substitute for cereal. They find it too dry and hard. Parents often ask whether they can offer their toddlers egg matzah instead. Small children who are finicky eaters generally find egg matzah more appealing and are more likely to accept it.

There is a difference of opinion as to whether adults are permitted to eat egg matzah on Pesach. Rabbi Yosef Caro states in the *Shulchan Aruch* that there is no restriction on eating this type of matzah,[15] as many Sephardic communities follow his decision.[16] Rema notes that the Ashkenazim consider egg matzah forbidden.

It is for sick or elderly people who require egg matzah that an exception can be made.[17] Obviously those Sephardim who follow the opinion of Rabbi Yosef Caro are permitted to feed small children egg matzah. However, even communities which accept the more stringent view of Rema (all Ashkenazim and some Sephardim) are permitted to feed egg matzah to toddlers. Small children are clearly comparable to the sick. In general, the halachic rule is that whatever may be done for the sick may be done for small children.[18] Rema himself notes that the old and the sick may be given egg matzah on Pesach. However, if the child will eat an adequate diet without the addition of egg matzah, the parent is not permitted to offer him this type of matzah on Pesach.

Bedikat Chametz

A Jew is required to search his home and property for chametz on the night of the thirteenth of Nisan in order to remove all chametz from his possession. This requirement is rabbinic in origin.[19] The obligation of performing bedikat chametz is not a personal one for each Jewish individual, and a homeowner may appoint a representative to search his house for chametz. If he does so, he is absolved of any further responsibility in regard to this mitzvah.[20] Despite this, the poskim recommend that the homeowner perform some of the search, since it is preferable to be personally involved in the mitzvah.[21] Now, since searching for chametz is not an individual personal obligation, parents are not required to have their children fulfill this mitzvah. Nevertheless, parents often wish to involve their children in the search for chametz. This is true for two reasons. In the first instance, parents wish to give their children a share in performing this mitzvah. Secondly, if the property which is to be searched is large, it is easier if some parts of it can be delegated to the children of the family as their duty. This lessens the burden on the parents. The question arises whether it is appropriate for parents to allow children to perform this function, since it is doubtful that a minor will do the thorough search for chametz required by Halachah. The *Shulchan Aruch* states that *ex post facto* (*di'eved*) one may accept the word of a child who has reached the age of chinuch that a particular area is free of chametz.[22] However, the poskim point out that in the first instance parents should not delegate such a task to a minor child. Searching for chametz is a job which involves concentration and great effort, and children cannot be trusted to do the job properly.[23] Therefore, if parents wish to have their minor children participate in searching for chametz, they must have an adult go over the areas searched by the children. However, if they fail to do this, they may *ex post facto* rely on the search performed by the children.

Erev Pesach

Erev Pesach, the day prior to Passover, has special requirements of its own. On this day it is customary for all *bechorim*, firstborn males, to fast. This is done in memory of the plague of the firstborn that occurred in Egypt on the Seder night and from which the Jewish firstborns were spared.[24] The *Shulchan Aruch* states that firstborn minors need not observe the fast. However, their parents are required to fast for them. If the father is not a *bechor*, he is required to fast for his firstborn son. When the father is a *bechor* and fasts to fulfill his own obligation, the mother is required to fast for her son.[25] Later authorities point out that in the latter case the mother is excused from the fast if observing it will cause her discomfort. Under these circumstances, the father's fast is counted for the son as well.[26] The prevailing practice today is for *bechorim* to attend a mitzvah meal, such as a *siyyum*, and thereby free themselves of the obligation to fast.[27] Fathers of firstborn sons are required to attend such a meal on Erev Pesach or else fast on behalf of their sons, even if they themselves are not *bechorim*.

A second law which applies to Erev Pesach is the prohibition of eating matzah on that day. This is forbidden so that the taste of matzah at the Seder will be fresh in one's mind.[28] Matzah products, such as matzah meal and items baked with matzah meal, are included in the prohibition.[29] Generally speaking, whenever an adult is forbidden to eat a certain food he is also not allowed to give it to a minor to eat. This prohibition, as mentioned earlier, begins with a child's birth. Since this is so using matzah products to feed babies should be forbidden on Erev Pesach, but the poskim note that it is permitted. Once the child is at an age where he is capable of understanding the story of Pesach and the meaning of matzah he may no longer be given these foods on Erev Pesach.[30] There are various reasons for this exception.[31] The prohibition of giving matzah or matzah products to children once they have reached the age of understanding applies both to boys and to girls. Since adult women are prohibited from eating such foods, the obligation of chinuch here applies to girls as well.[32]

The Seder

The highlight of the holiday of Pesach is, of course, the Seder. There are many mitzvot associated with the Seder. Certainly one of the central mitzvot of the evening is the recitation of the story of the Exodus from Egypt. The obligation to tell this story is a Torah duty for every Jew.[33] We fulfill this requirement by the reading of the Haggadah during the course of the Seder. The obligation to recite the account of the Exodus exists irrespective of whether or not one has children. If no children are present, adults are required to tell one another about these events. Nevertheless, the optimum fulfillment of this mitzvah is achieved when parents are able to tell the story of the Exodus to their children rather than to anyone else.[34]

In the case of this mitzvah the requirement of chinuch obligates parents to have their children present at the Seder and tell them the story of the evening. This obligation begins from the age at which the child is mature enough to understand at least part of the story of Pesach. The narration to the child should be determined by the child's intellectual level. A very young child should simply be told that all Jews were slaves in Egypt, and God redeemed them on this night. More details should be added as the child gets older and more capable of understanding, until finally the entire narration of the Haggadah can be told.[35] There is no difference between boys and girls in regard to this requirement. Parents are obligated to teach both about the redemption from Egypt.[36] Special efforts should be made to make sure that children are able to understand the Haggadah reading. Rema advocates that the entire recitation should be translated into the vernacular in order to achieve this goal.[37]

The rabbis of the Mishnah wanted to ensure that the Haggadah would be read as an answer to questions asked by children. This is the reason for the formulation of Mah Nishtanah in the form of four questions. Once a child is old enough to read Mah Nishtanah, he or she should be taught the words of this passage.[38] In addition, parents are required to encourage a questioning frame of mind in their child on the night of the Seder. If put in this state of mind, the child will hopefully come to spontaneously ask about the differences which separate this night from all other nights. In order to do this, parents should distribute nuts and candies to their children at the start of the Seder. This will stimulate their curiosity and encourage them to begin asking questions.[39] Some poskim endorse the custom of having the afikomen stolen as a similar method of stimulating curiosity on the part of children at the Seder.[40] In order to make sure that children's minds stay alert during the Seder, parents are required to begin the Seder immediately after nightfall. One should delay as little as possible.[41] Children must be allowed to stay up at the Seder until they hear at least a partial answer to the questions of the evening. They should not be sent to bed immediately after reciting Mah Nishtanah. At a minimum, parents should keep them up until the next paragraph, Avadim Hayeenu, is read and explained to them.[42]

The second major mitzvah of the Seder is the eating of matzah. This commandment is a Torah law which is binding on all Jewish adults, both male and female.[43] The minimum amount of matzah that must be eaten to fulfill this mitzvah is one *ke-*

zayit—the amount of an olive. However, the *Shulchan Aruch* prescribes that four such amounts of matzah must be consumed during the Seder. At the initial eating of the matzah two *kezaytim* should be consumed. Then at Korech a *kezayit* of matzah should be combined with maror, and finally one *kezayit* of matzah should be eaten as the afikomen at the end of the meal.[44] When a boy or girl is old enough to remain awake for the Seder and eat these quantities of matzah, parents are required by the mitzvah of chinuch to see to it that their child fulfills these requirements. Even when the child is too young to do this, parents should at least make sure that the child eats one *kezayit* of matzah on the night of the Seder.[45] By doing this, the parents ensure that their child fulfills the actual Torah requirement of eating matzah. This is true because all opinions agree that an adult who disregards the extra amounts of matzah prescribed by the *Shulchan Aruch* and eats only one *kezayit* fulfills thereby the mitzvah of eating matzah on Pesach.[46]

Another requirement of the Seder is the drinking of four cups of wine. This obligation presents a problem because it is difficult for young children to consume such a large quantity of wine. The *Shulchan Aruch* states that it is advisable to give children who have reached the age of understanding four cups of wine at the appropriate places during the Seder.[47] This age will differ according to the maturity of the child.[48] The cups given to the children should be large enough to contain a *revi'it* of wine.[49] The size of a *revi'it* is subject to debate. Rabbi Moshe Feinstein states that this amount is, at a minimum, the equivalent of 3.3 ounces.[50] Small decorative cups that do not hold this quantity of liquid should obviously not be used. Some authorities advise that even children below the age of chinuch should have a cup of wine placed before them at the Seder. In this case, the cup used may be quite small and need not contain a *revi'it*.[51] It is unclear whether parents are required to abide by this opinion.[52]

It should be noted that even children above the age of chinuch are not required to drink most of the contents of each one of their cups. It is sufficient if they consume *melo' lugmov* of the cup. This is the equivalent of the amount of wine necessary to make the child's cheek bulge if the wine was all concentrated on one side of his mouth. This means that each child is required to drink from his Seder cup an amount appropriate to the size of his mouth.[53] There is no difference between boys and girls in this respect. Parents are obligated to have all their children fulfill this mitzvah.[54]

There is no question but that grape juice may be substituted for wine in the four cups given to children.[55] It should further be noted that in cases of difficulty parents may totally forgo the giving of the four cups to children who are past the age of chinuch. Many poskim argue that this obligation does not apply to children at all. Parents should attempt to have children fulfill this mitzvah, but if they cannot do so no clear violation of Halachah occurs.[56]

The mitzvah of chinuch, of course, applies to all other requirements of the Seder as well. Adults, both male and female, are obligated to eat a *kezayit* of maror at the Seder.[57] This is a rabbinic requirement rather than a Torah one.[58] Nevertheless, parents are required to have both boys and girls past the age of understanding fulfill this mitzvah. There is a duty of chinuch for rabbinic mitzvot just as there is for Torah mitzvot.[59] A second rabbinic requirement of the Seder is that the four cups of wine and the matzah be eaten while in a reclining position.[60] Here again, parents are obligated by the duty of chinuch to teach their children to fulfill this mitzvah. Adult women are not required to eat or drink in this position.[61] It therefore follows that only boys need to be taught to do this. Girls are exempt, since as adults they will not be obligated to observe this mitzvah.

Sefirat HaOmer

The holiday of Pesach is followed by the festival of Shavuot. The two holidays are linked together by the mitzvah of Sefirat

HaOmer, the couting of the Omer. This mitzvah is a binding obligation on all Jewish men. Women are exempt from it because it is a positive mitzvah dependent on time. *Magen Avraham* observes that women have nonetheless accepted this obligation on themselves and customarily count the Omer.[62] The Chafetz Chaim states that in his locale women did not fulfill this mitzvah. He argues that even if women wish to count the Omer they should not make the berachah on the mitzvah because they probably will make a mistake in their count.[63] The majority of poskim, however, agree with *Magen Avraham* that it is appropriate for women to fulfill the mitzvah and make the blessing over it.[64] This is because even when women are exempt from a mitzvah they commit no sin by voluntarily fulfilling it and reciting a berachah.[65] This position is not accepted by the Sephardic Acharonim. They argue that women are permitted to voluntarily fulfill mitzvot from which they are exempt but may not make a berachah before performing such mitzvot. Women of Sephardic communities are therefore permitted to count the Omer if they so wish, but not to pronounce the berachah over it.[66]

The obligation of chinuch in regard to this mitzvah depends on the preceding discussion. There is no doubt that parents are required to teach boys, from the age of understanding, to count the Omer. It is similarly clear that there is no such obligation for girls. If parents, nevertheless, wish to teach their daughters to perform this mitzvah, there is a question as to whether they should allow them to make the berachah over the Omer. Those following *Magen Avraham* will permit this, while those disagreeing would forbid it. In all cases, Sephardic families should not teach their daughters to pronounce the blessing.

There is a second question in regard to this mitzvah. If a person misses one day out of the counting of the Omer he is not permitted to continue counting with a berachah.[67] There is doubt as to how this applies to a boy who becomes bar mitzvah during the days of the Omer count. Here the boy's counting prior to his bar mitzvah was not done as the fulfillment of a personal obligation, since he was a minor at the time. It was done only as a matter of chinuch. Some poskim argue that since this is so, the boy is not permitted to count the remainder of the Omer days with a berachah. It is considered as if the boy missed part of the counting of the Omer.[68] Other authorities disagree, pointing out that the boy counted the preceding days as a fulfillment of the mitzvah of chinuch. This is sufficient to consider it as if all the days have been counted. He may therefore continue to count the Omer after his bar mitzvah with a berachah.[69]

The Three Weeks of Mourning

During the summer season Jews are required to observe three weeks of mourning in commemoration of the destruction of the Beit HaMikdash. This period commences with the fast of Shiva Asar BeTammuz, the seventeenth of Tammuz, and ends with the fast of Tisha B'Av, the ninth of Av, exactly three weeks later. Besides the fast-days themselves, which begin and end this period, all the days within this period have special restrictions of varying degrees. Parents often have questions as to how far these restrictions should be applied to children.

The fast-days themselves, both these two and others during the year, have as their primary restriction the prohibition on eating and drinking. This prohibition applies to both men and women who are physically capable of fasting.[70] There is, however, no requirement of chinuch in regard to this mitzvah. Children below the age of bar mitzvah or bat mitzvah are not required to go without nourishment on any fast-day.[71] Indeed, it is wrong to allow them to do so even if they wish to.[72] Furthermore, with the exception of Yom Kippur, parents are not required to have their children go without food for even a short period of time on any fast-day.[73] There is, however, one restriction which does apply to children on all fast-days. On these days parents should only feed simple foods to children who have reached the age of understanding. Delicacies or specially tasty things should be avoided. In this way, the child is educated to take part in the fasting of the adult community. No such restriction applies to children too young to understand what a fast-day is.[74]

Ashkenazic practice is for adults to refrain from haircutting during the entire three weeks of mourning.[75] Some Acharonim are of the opinion that parents must also refrain from cutting children's hair for this entire period. This requirement results from the parent's duty of chinuch.[76] Others disagree and argue that in the case of children this is only forbidden during the actual week in which Tisha B'Av occurs. Prior to that time haircutting may be done.[77] Both opinions agree that when this prohibition applies, even children below the age of understanding should not have their hair cut.[78]

Ashkenazic communities also refrain from attending musical events or programs for the entire three-week period.[79] Despite this, children may be taken to sports events or programs where music is incidental. This is even permitted during the nine days of mourning immediately prior to Tisha B'Av. Of course, actual concerts or musical performances should be avoided.[80]

For the first nine days of the month of Av, Ashkenzic practice forbids both the laundering of clothing[81] and the wearing of freshly washed clothes.[82] These restrictions do not apply to small children. Rema states that infants' clothes, which continually get dirty as the child wears them, may be washed during this time. Even the clothing of older children may be washed during these days.[83] Some poskim say that it is only permissible to wash the clothing of children up to the age of about three. Once the child is past that age, washing may no longer be done.[84] Other poskim do not make this distinction. They permit all children's clothing to be washed during these days.[85] The prohibitions on washing children's clothing and giving them freshly washed clothes are similar to the restriction on cutting their hair. Some authorities say that when this is prohibited one may not do it for the entire period of the nine days.[86] Other say that it is only forbidden during the week in which Tisha B'Av occurs.[87] It should be noted that even when one is permitted to wash children's clothes during this time, an effort should be made to do so in a private location. A laundromat or other public place should be avoided if possible.[88]

Ashkenazic communities observe an additional prohibition during the first nine days of the month of Av. No bathing is permitted for either men or women during this time. This includes bathing in both hot and cold water.[89] Washing oneself for health reasons, to remove dirt and perspiration, is allowed.[90] Some poskim allow children below bar mitzvah or bat mitzvah to bathe in cold water or go swimming during these days.[91] Others forbid this in public, but allow children to be bathed in this manner in private.[92] There is certainly no prohibition on bathing children when this is done for health reasons, as is usually the case.

There is a further prohibition on eating meat and drinking wine during these nine days.[93] It would seem that since parents are forbidden to give prohibited food to children of all ages, they should not be allowed to feed these foods to their children during this time. *Magen Avraham*, however, argues that it is permissible during the nine days to give meat and wine to children below the age of understanding. His proof is from the fact that the *Shulchan Aruch* permits giving the wine of Havdalah during this time to such small children.[94] Other poskim claim that parents may only give such food to toddlers and small children when this is done for the purpose of a mitzvah, such as Havdalah, but not otherwise.[95] Some Acharonim decide in accordance with *Magen Avraham*,[96] while others agree with the more stringent opinion.[97] According to all opinions a toddler or small child who insists on eating meat and will not be adequately nourished otherwise may be given meat to eat. Indeed, even an adult who cannot subsist on a dairy diet is permitted to eat poultry during these days.[98] On the other hand, it is equally clear that children who have reached the age of understanding may not be given meat, wine, or grape juice during this period. Parents are bound by the mitzvah of chinuch to train them to observe this restriction.[99] Here again, if an older child refuses dairy foods and is in danger of actual malnutrition, poultry may be used.[100]

The fast of Tisha B'Av itself has a number of special prohibitions. On that day it is forbidden to learn Torah except for mournful or sad subjects. The reason for this is that the study of Torah makes one happy.[101] Parents are required by the mitzvah of chinuch to train older children who can study on their own not to study Torah on Tisha B'Av. This is true because Torah study makes older children happy just as it does adults.[102] Similarly, parents should not teach Torah to smaller children on Tisha B'Av. There is an argument among the poskim as to whether parents may teach children those Torah subjects which an adult is permitted to study on Tisha B'Av. *Magen Avraham* states that this is forbidden, since teaching Torah in any form is prohibited on Tisha B'Av.[103] Other authorities disagree. They permit parents to teach children anything which the parents themselves may learn on this day.[104] Even *Magen Avraham* agrees that parents may give their children a simple narration of the events associated with the destruction of the Beit HaMikdash[105]

The requirement of fasting on Tisha B'Av does not apply to children, as mentioned earlier. A disagreement exists, however, in regard to the other prohibitions of the day. On Tisha B'Av adults are forbidden to wear leather shoes.[106] It would seem that the duty of chinuch requires parents to train children who have reached the age of understanding to observe this restriction. Nevertheless, *Chochmat Adam* states that it is not necessary to do this. His reason is that parents are not obligated by the duty of chinuch to do something which results in discomfort for their child[107] Rabbi Moshe Feinstein disagrees. He writes that parents are required to see to it that their children observe all the restrictions of Tisha B'Av as a fulfillment of their duty of chinuch. This refers not only to the wearing of non-leather shoes, but also to the prohibitions of washing and anointing oneself on Tisha B'Av. Of course, this does not apply to small children below the age of chinuch.[108]

Rosh Hashanah and Yom Kippur

The central observance of Rosh Hashanah is the blowing of the shofar. The obligation to hear the shofar is a Torah requirement for men.[109] Since this mitzvah is a positive commandment related to time, women are not obligated to observe it. Nevertheless, it is appropriate for women to fulfill this mitzvah and they are rewarded for so doing.[110] There is no doubt that the duty of chinuch obligates parents to make sure that their sons hear the shofar blowing.[111] There is no such requirement in regard to girls, because adult women are not obligated to hear the shofar, but it is appropriate to accustom girls to hearing the shofar since adult women fulfill a voluntary mitzvah by doing this.

If children have missed the shofar blowing in the synagogue an adult should sound the shofar for them a second time. No violation of Yom Tov occurs when this is done, since the mitzvah of chinuch is being fulfilled.[112] Some poskim hold that the shofar may not be carried through a public domain on Yom Tov in order to sound it for children even though it would be permitted for adults.[113] Others, however, permit this to be done for the purpose of the mitzvah of chinuch.[114]

All of this applies to children who have reached the age of understanding. Parents of children below that age have no such obligation. The poskim urge that such small children not be brought to the shofar blowing, if at all possible, since they will disturb adults who are attempting to fulfill the mitzvah. If there is no place to leave them, they should be kept in the women's section of the synagogue. In this way, if they do disturb adults they will not stop men, who are actually obligated to hear the shofar, from fulfilling their obligation.[115] Some synagogues provide babysitting for small children during the shofar blowing. This enables both the mothers and the fathers to fulfill this important mitzvah.

All Jewish adults are obligated by Torah law to refrain from food and drink during the course of Yom Kippur.[116] The duty of chinuch applies to this mitzvah in a limited fashion. Children under the age of nine or ten should not refrain from eating on Yom Kippur, even for a short amount of time.[117] Children below this age frequently beg for permission to fast an hour or two on Yom Kippur, but parents must not allow them to do so.[118] This prohibition applies to a healthy child below the age of nine and a weak child below the age of ten.[119] No change in such a young child's normal eating schedule is permitted, so parents are halachically required to have food with them in the synagogue to give their young children during the course of the day or to make sure that they go home and eat at the proper time.[120] Boys older than nine and girls over ten should be trained not to eat at their regular meal times on Yom Kippur. Their eating should be delayed for an increasing number of hours as they get older, but not for the whole day.[121] This applies to both boys and girls.[122] Unless a parent has been informed by a doctor that the child can fast the entire day without any ill effect, the child should not fast even if the child requests this.[123]

When boys and girls reach the age of eleven, according to the *Shulchan Aruch*, they should be trained to fast the entire day of Yom Kippur as a fulfillment of the duty of chinuch.[124] Rema adds that if the child is weak or sickly, this is not necessary. The parents may then continue to have the child fast for only a number of hours on Yom Kippur.[125] Many poskim disagree with this stringent position. They state that parents are not required under any circumstances to have their children below bar or bat mitzvah fast an entire day of Yom Kippur. They reason that all children today are considered to be in the category of the weak or the sickly who are not required to attempt an all-day fast. Parents consequently fulfill the obligation of chinuch even with these children by having them abstain from food for a few hours on Yom Kippur.[126] Although some authorities argue for the more stringent view,[127] the majority of Acharonim accept the lenient opinion.[128]

There are additional prohibitions. On this day adult Jews may not wash any part of their bodies,[129] anoint their skin,[130] or wear leather shoes.[131] The poskim agree that parents are obligated to see to it that their children observe these restriction on Yom Kippur.[132] Even if children are below the age of understanding—even from birth—parents may not wash them or dress them in leather shoes on this day, since by doing so they would be actively causing the children to commit a prohibited act.[133] However, it is always permitted to wash away actual dirt with water on Yom Kippur. It is therefore clear that parents may clean a child who has soiled himself on this day.[134] It should be noted that chinuch on Yom Kippur differs from other fast-days in regard to one point. Parents are not required to have their children refrain from eating delicacies on Yom Kippur, as they are on other fast-days. This is because Yom Kippur is a festival and not a day of mourning.[135]

Sukkot

The holiday of Sukkot has two central mitzvot. The first of these observances is the requirement to dwell in the sukkah. In order to fulfill this mitzvah in its complete sense the Jew is required to spend as much of his time as possible in the sukkah. However, as a minimum he is obligated to eat all of his meals throughout the holiday in that location.[136] This mitzvah, since it is a positive commandment which is time-oriented, applies to men but not to women, but women may observe the mitzvah and pronounce the berachah over it, if they wish to.[137]

Parents are required to ensure that their sons eat their meals in the sukkah beginning, according to the *Shulchan Aruch*, from five or six years of age.[138] *Magen Avraham* explains that if a boy is bright and understands the meaning of the sukkah, this requirement begins at the age of five, while if he is less intellectually mature it begins at the age of six.[139] Other authorities state that if the boy is precocious, the parents are required to have him eat his meals in the sukkah from the age of four. If he is not intellectually advanced, they can wait until the age of five or six. In the latter case, if the boy's father lives with him permanently he is required to have his son eat in the sukkah from the age of five. Only if the father is absent from home most of the year can the parents wait until the boy is six before making him eat his meals in the sukkah.[140] The majority of poskim agree with *Magen Avraham*'s opinion,[141] although a minority recommend that the more stringent view be followed.[142] According to this majority opinion, parents are required to have their sons eat in the sukkah from the age of five or six. While it is common for parents not to insist on this, there is little jusitification for this attitude.[143] Since women are not required to eat in the sukkah as adults, there is no obligation for parents to accustom their daughters to observe this mitzvah as a fulfillment of chinuch. However, as is true of other mitzvot, parents are permitted to train girls to fulfill this obligation and make a berachah over it should they so choose.

The second basic mitzvah of Sukkot is the taking of the *arba minim*, the four species, which include the etrog and lulav. This requirement is also binding on adult men but not women.[144] The Mishnah states that a minor boy who knows how to follow the proper procedure in waving the four species is required to observe this mitzvah.[144] The *Shulchan Aruch* understands this to mean that parents are obligated to buy a set of the four species for their minor son as a fulfillment of the responsibility of chinuch. This purchase is independent of, and in addition to, the *arba minim* bought by the father to fulfill his personal mitzvah.[146] This obligation begins when the boy is mature enough to be able to properly wave the *arba minim*. If he is unable to do this, the parent has no such requirement. In that case there is no obligation to even teach the boy to make the berachah over the four species.[147] Once a boy is able to wave the *arba minim* in the prescribed six directions, even though he does not perform the procedure in all its details, parents are obligated to purchase the set for him.[148] Of course, no such requirement exists for daughters, since women are exempt from this mitzvah.

The position of the *Shulchan Aruch* is contested by Maharshal. He argues that parents are only required by the mitzvah of chinuch to have their sons make the blessing over the *arba minim* and wave them. This can be done by the father giving his species to his son after he is finished using them. It is not necessary for parents to purchase an individual set of the *minim* for a minor son.[149] *Turei Zahav* suggests that the correct procedure is for parents to buy a separate set of the *minim* for a minor son if they have the means to afford it. By so doing they fulfill the mitzvah of chinuch in its highest form. Only if they are unable to absorb the financial cost should they rely on the argument of Maharshal.[150] This opinion is quoted approvingly by later poskim.[151] Rabbi Moshe Feinstein states that in contemporary America, where true poverty is extremely rare, there is no justification for relying on the opinion of Maharshal. Thus parents are required to purchase sets of *arba minim* for their minor sons.[152]

Naturally when parents purchase the *minim* for a minor as a fulfillment of chinuch, they are required to buy a fully kosher set.[153] It is common today for species which are not even minimally kosher to be sold with the name "chinuch sets." Unfortunately, parents who purchase these sets do not thereby fulfill the mitzvah of chinuch. However, as long as the *minim* bought for minors are kosher, there is no obligation to pay more for a superior set. This is because the duty of chinuch only pertains to the mandatory part of a mitzvah and not to *hiddur mitzvah*, questions which involve the best manner of performing a mitzvah versus the less preferred way.[154]

If parents rely on the lenient opinion and give a minor boy the family's *minim* to make a berachah over, another problem exists. The taking of the four species is a Torah requirement on the first day of Sukkot. It is only a rabbinic mitzvah for the remainder of the holiday.[155] In order for the Torah obligation to be fulfilled, the species must be the legal possession of the person using them. To satisfy this requirement, a person who borrows someone's etrog and lulav on the first day of Sukkot receives them as a present and then returns them to their former owner after using them.[156] The *Shulchan Aruch* notes that a minor has the halachic ability to take something into his possession but not to return it to its original owner. Therefore on the first day of Sukkot, it advises that a father should not give his set to his minor son before he himself has performed the mitzvah. If he is not careful about this he will be unable to use the etrog and lulav for himself, since they will not be his legal possession once his son has used them.[157]

The poskim point out that there is a further complication for Jews living outside of Israel. In areas where two days of Yom Tov are observed, the second day must be treated exactly as the first. This means that even after a father performs his mitzvah with the *minim* on the first day, he will still be unable to give them to his son. If he lets his son take them, he will be unable to use them for himself on the second day of the holiday. This is so because the species will not be his legal possession.[158] Some authorities state that in such a case the father should hold the species together with the son when the boy performs the mitzvah. In this way the father does not surrender his legal ownership, but still fulfills the mitzvah of chinuch with his son.[159] The majority of poskim, however, state that by doing this the father does not satisfy the obligation of chinuch. This is because the son has not become the legal owner of the *minim* at the time he performs the mitzvah.[160] There are other suggestions offered by the poskim to avoid this difficulty.[161] It is due to this problem that Rabbi Moshe Feinstein writes that in contemporary America parents are required to buy individual sets of *minim* for their minor sons.[162]

A minor boy can never be called to the Torah for any aliyah other than Maftir throughout the year. There is, however, one exception to this rule. On Simchat Torah it is customary to give aliyot to everyone present in the synagogue, so that all can share in the joy of completing the reading of the Torah,[163] including all the boys, who come up together for the next-to-last aliyah, before Chatan Torah.[164] One boy makes the blessing for all those assembled, while another makes the concluding berachah on behalf of all. If the boys are incapable of doing this, an adult leads them in these blessings.[165] After their Torah reading is over, before the final blessing is made, the children are blessed with the words of Genesis 48:16, beginning with the words *Hamalach hagoel.*[166]

Chanukah

The major observance of the festival of Chanukah is the requirement to light the menorah every night. This obligation is satisfied in strict halachic terms when the head of the household kindles just one flame every evening of Chanukah.[167] Universally however, it is the custom to light one additional flame for each new night of the holiday. Rabbi Yosef Caro states that only one menorah should be lit in a house. The individual members of the family should not kindle their own menorahs. Rema disagrees, writing that the accepted practice is for each member of the household to light his own menorah.[168] Sephardic practice follows Rabbi Yosef Caro, while the Ashkenazim act in accordance with Rema.[169]

The difference between the two groups determines whether or not an obligation of chinuch exists in regard to this mitzvah. Sephardic parents are not required to teach minors to light the menorah, because in Sephardic practice the mitzvah is not meant for each individual, but is left exclusively to the head of the household.[170] On the other hand, according to Ashkenazic procedure it seems that parents would be required to have their children light the menorah, since each individual adult performs the mitzvah. This is, indeed, the opinion of Rema.[171] *Magen Avraham*, however, argues that this is incorrect. Since the Ashkenazic custom of having every individual light the menorah is merely a fulfillment of *hiddur mitzvah*, the best manner of performing a mitzvah, rather than the actual mitzvah itself, chinuch does not apply to it.[172] Some authorities seem to agree with *Magen Avraham*.[173] Despite this, the current custom is to have minor boys, from the age of chinuch, each light an individual menorah.[174] The same practice does not hold for girls, even though single adult women are required to kindle the menorah. Various reasons are given to justify this.[175]

Purim

The main mitzvah of Purim is, of course, the reading of Megillat Esther. The obligation to hear the Megillah on Purim applies to both men and women.[176] This requirement is a dual one. One must hear the Megillah on Purim night and again during the day.[177] Parents are obligated by the duty of chinuch to see to it that their children attend both Megillah readings.[178] This requirement applies equally to both boys and girls.[179] However, there is no such obligation in regard to children below the age of chinuch. Children who are so young should not be brought to the Megillah reading, lest they make noise and disturb the adults present who wish to hear the Megillah.[180] When older children are brought to the Megillah reading, parents should make sure that their purpose in coming is to hear the Megillah and not exclusively to make noise at the mention of the name of Haman.[181]

The other mitzvot of Purim include *matanot la'evyonim*, gifts to the poor, and *mishloach manot*, sending portions of food to friends. These mitzvot apply equally to both men and women.[182] The duty of chinuch obligates parents to have their children, both boys and girls, fulfill these mitzvot. This requirement begins when the children reach the age of chinuch, as with all other mitzvot.[183] A widespread minhag exists of giving a *machtzit hashekel*, three half-shekels, to charity on the eve of Purim. This donation is in memory of the half-shekel given in ancient times for maintenance of the Temple. It consists of three halves of the major coin of the time and place.[184] Some authorities say that these coins should be given for each male family member, including minor boys from birth onwards.[185] *Magen Avraham* disagrees, claiming that there is no such custom for boys below the age of bar mitzvah.[186] Later poskim note that contemporary practice follows *Magen Avraham*.[187] According to all opinions, if parents have voluntarily begun to donate *machtzit hashekel* for their minor sons, then it is obligatory for them to continue doing so. In such a case this becomes a binding vow on the parents.[188]

Yom Tov and Chol Hamoed

Jews are under a Torah obligation to rejoice on Yom Tov. This means that they must do things to put themselves in a happy frame of mind on these days. The head of a family is required to make sure that all members of his household participate in the mitzvah of rejoicing on festivals. The Talmud states that a father should buy candies and other treats for his children on Yom Tov in order to fulfill this obligation.[189] The *Shulchan Aruch* codifies this as binding halachah today.[190]

The intermediate days of Passover and Sukkot are known as Chol Hamoed. Many types of work are forbidden on these days, while others are permitted. Both haircutting and washing of clothes are generally prohibited on Chol Hamoed.[191] It would seem that parents are bound by their duty of chinuch not to cut the hair of their children or wash their clothes on these days. This is, however, not so. The *Shulchan Aruch* states that parents may cut their children's hair on Chol Hamoed.[192] *Magen Avraham* explains that this is so because the child was free of any obligation to have his hair cut prior to the festival. He adds, however, that this should only be done when the hair is very long and causes the child discomfort.[193] Later poskim agree with this position. Except for cases of discomfort, haircutting should not be done for children during Chol Hamoed.[194]

The prohibition of washing clothes causes great problems for parents of small children. Such children soil their clothes frequently and cannot go for eight or nine days without having their garments washed. The *Shulchan Aruch* states that children's clothing which gets dirty frequently may be washed on Chol Hamoed since the child is considered to be like a person without enough clothing to wear through the holiday. However, it cautions that such garments should be washed one at a time.[195] Diapers and other clothing used by infants are not included in this ruling. A number of these items may be washed together since many of them are needed at the same time.[196] Modern poskim agree that nowadays, when children's clothes are changed daily and washed by machine rather than by hand, these differences no longer hold true. The clothing of infants and older small children may be washed in one batch on Chol Hamoed as long as care is taken not to wash more articles of clothing than will be needed for the festival.[197]

Notes

1. משנה תורה, הלכות חמץ ומצה פרק א׳, הלכות א׳, ב׳.
2. מגן אברהם סימן שמ״ג, ס״ק ג׳.
3. פרי מגדים, אשל אברהם שם.
4. מגן אברהם שם.
5. מגן אברהם סימן ת״נ, ס״ק ח׳, משנה ברורה שם, ס״ק י״ח.
6. מגן אברהם שם.
7. חק יעקב שם ס״ק י״א, ערוך השולחן שם, סעיף י״ד.
8. חיי אדם כלל קכ״ד, סעיף כ״א, משנה ברורה סימן ת״נ, ס״ק י״ח.
9. ערוך השולחן סימן ת״נ, סעיף י״ד.
10. משנה ברורה שם.
11. מגן אברהם, סימן שמ״ג, ס״ק ג׳, משנה ברורה שם, ס״ק ד׳.
12. אורח חיים סימן תנ״ג, סעיף א׳.
13. שם, ברמ״א.
14. חיי אדם, כלל קכ״ז, סעיף א׳, משנה ברורה סימן תנ״ג, ס״ק ז׳.
15. אורח חיים סימן תס״ב, סעיף ד׳.
16. כף החיים שם, ס״ק ל״ח, מ״א.
17. אורח חיים סימן תס״ב, סעיף ד׳, רמ״א שם.
18. אורח חיים סימן שכ״ח, סעיף י״ז ברמ״א.
19. מגן אברהם, סימן תל״א, ס״ק ב׳.
20. אורח חיים סימן תל״ב, סעיף ב׳.
21. מגן אברהם שם ס״ק ה׳, חק יעקב שם, ס״ק י׳.
22. אורח חיים סימן תל״ז, סעיף ד׳.
23. מגן אברהם שם ס״ק ח׳, משנה ברורה שם, ס״ק י״ח.
24. טור אורח חיים, סימן ת״ע, שולחן ערוך שם, סעיף א׳.
25. שם, סעיף ב׳, ברמ״א.
26. מגן אברהם שם, ס״ק ב׳, משנה ברורה שם, ס״ק ט׳.
27. משנה ברורה שם, ס״ק י׳.
28. טור אורח חיים סימן תע״א, שולחן ערוך שם, סעיף ב׳ ברמ״א.

29. שולחן ערוך שם.
30. שולחן ערוך שם.
31. מגן אברהם שם, ס"ק ז', מחצית השקל שם.
32. מחצית השקל שם, משנה ברורה שם, ס"ק י"ג.
33. משנה תורה, הלכות חמץ ומצה, פרק ז', הלכה א'.
34. שם, הלכה ג', אורח חיים, סימן תע"ג, סעיף ז'.
35. משנה תורה שם, הלכה ג'.
36. משנה ברורה, סימן תע"ג, ס"ק ס"ד.
37. אורח חיים, סימן תע"ג, סעיף ו' ברמ"א, משנה ברורה שם ס"ק ס"ג.
38. אורח חיים שם, סעיף ז'.
39. משנה תורה, הלכות חמץ ומצה, פרק ז', הלכה ג', אורח חיים, סימן תע"ב, סעיף ט"ז, משנה ברורה שם, ס"ק נ'.
40. משנה תורה שם, חק יעקב, סימן תע"ב, ס"ק ב'.
41. אורח חיים סימן תע"ב, סעיף א', משנה ברורה שם, ס"ק ג', ד'.
42. משנה ברורה שם, ס"ק נ'.
43. אורח חיים שם, סעיף י"ד, משנה ברורה שם, ס"ק מ"ה.
44. אורח חיים, סימן תע"ה, סעיף א', סימן תע"ז, סעיף א'. Some poskim recommend that two *kezaytim* of matzah be eaten as the afikomen. See משנה ברורה, סימן תע"ז, ס"ק א'
45. משנה תורה, הלכות חמץ ומצה, פרק ו', הלכה י'.
46. שולחן ערוך הגרש"ז, סימן תע"ה, סעיף ח'.
47. אורח חיים, סימן תע"ב, סעיף ט"ו.
48. פרי מגדים, אשל אברהם, שם, ס"ק ט"ו.
49. חק יעקב שם, ס"ק כ"ז.
50. הגדה קול דודי, פרק ב', ס"ק ו'.
51. חק יעקב, סימן תע"ב, ס"ק כ"ז.
52. חזון עובדיה, הלכות סדר ליל פסח, קדש, ס"ק ג'.
53. משנה ברורה, סימן תע"ב, ס"ק מ"ז.
54. אורח חיים שם, סעיף י"ד, ערוך השולחן שם, סעיף ט"ו.
55. שערים המצויינים בהלכה, סימן ק"ח, ס"ק א'.
56. משנה ברורה, סימן תע"ב, ס"ק מ"ו, שער הציון שם, ס"ק ס'.
57. אורח חיים, סימן תע"ה, סעיף א', סימן תע"ב, סעיף י"ד.
58. משנה תורה, הלכות חמץ ומצה, פרק ז', הלכה י"ב.
59. משנה ברורה, סימן שמ"ג, ס"ק ג'.
60. משנה תורה, הלכות חמץ ומצה, פרק ז', הלכות ו', ז'.
61. אורח חיים, סימן תע"ב, סעיף ד'.
62. מגן אברהם, סימן תפ"ט, ס"ק א'.
63. משנה ברורה שם, ס"ק ג'.
64. חק יעקב שם, ס"ק ג', אליה רבה שם, ס"ק ב', שולחן ערוך הגרש"ז שם, סעיף ב'.
65. שולחן ערוך הגרש"ז שם.

66. כף החיים, שם, ס"ק ט'.
67. אורח חיים שם, סעיף ח'.
68. ברכי יוסף שם, ס"ק כ'.
69. שערי תשובה שם, ס"ק כ'.
70. אורח חיים, סימן תק"נ, סעיף א'.
71. מגן אברהם שם, ס"ק ב'.
72. שו"ת מנחם עזריה, סימן ק"יא.
73. משנה ברורה, סימן תק"נ, ס"ק ה'.
74. מגן אברהם שם, ס"ק ב', משנה ברורה שם, ס"ק ה'.
75. אורח חיים, סימן תקנ"א, סעיף ד', ברמ"א.
76. אליה רבה שם, ס"ק ל"א.
77. חיי אדם, כלל קל"ג, סעיף י"ח.
78. חיי אדם שם, משנה ברורה, סימן תקנ"א, ס"ק פ"א, שער הציון שם, ס"ק צ"א.
79. משנה ברורה שם, ס"ק ט"ז.
80. דעת הגר"מ פיינשטיין הובא בספר מועדי ישורון מאת הרב פעלדער, פרק ה', סעיף א', ס"ק ו', סעיף ב', ס"ק ל"ח.
81. אורח חיים, סימן תקנ"א, סעיף ג', ברמ"א.
82. שם, סעיף ט"ז, ברמ"א.
83. שם, סעיף י"ד, ברמ"א.
84. חיי אדם, כלל קל"ג, סעיף י"ח, כף החיים, סימן תקנ"א, ס"ק קע"ט.
85. פרי מגדים, אשל אברהם, סימן תקנ"א, ס"ק ל"ט.
86. אליה רבה שם, ס"ק ל"א.
87. חיי אדם, כלל קל"ג, סעיף י"ח.
88. מגן אברהם, סימן תקנ"א, ס"ק ל"ח, משנה ברורה, שם, ס"ק פ"ג.
89. אורח חיים, סימן תקנ"א, סעיף ט"ז, ברמ"א.
90. ערוך השולחן שם, סעיף ל"ז, דעת הגר"מ פיינשטיין מובא בספר מועדי ישורון, פרק ה', סעיף ב', ס"ק י"ח, י"ט.
91. שו"ת רבבות אפרים, אורח חיים, חלק ב', סימן קנ"ה.
92. שערים המצויינים בהלכה, קונטרס אחרון, סימן קכ"ב, ס"ק י"ב.
93. אורח חיים סימן תקנ"א, סעיף ט' ברמ"א.
94. מגן אברהם שם, ס"ק ל"א.
95. דגול מרבבה שם, אליה רבה שם, ס"ק כ"ד.
96. חיי אדם, כלל קל"ג, סעיף ט"ז.
97. משנה ברורה, סימן תקנ"א, ס"ק ע'.
98. משנה ברורה שם, ס"ק ס"ד, ערוך השולחן שם, סעיף כ"ו.
99. שו"ת אגרות משה, יורה דעה, חלק א', סימן רכ"ד.
100. משנה ברורה, סימן תקנ"א, ס"ק ס"ד, ערוך השולחן שם, סעיף כ"ו.
101. אורח חיים, סימן תקנ"ד, סעיף א'.
102. ביאור הלכה שם, ד"ה „בטלים".

103. מגן אברהם שם, ס"ק ב'.
104. ט"ז שם, ס"ק א', דגול מרבבה שם.
105. מגן אברהם שם.
106. אורח חיים שם, סעיף ט"ז.
107. חכמת אדם, כלל קל"ב, סעיף י"ז.
108. שו"ת אגרות משה, יורה דעה, חלק א', סימן רכ"ד.
109. משנה תורה, הלכות שופר, פרק ב', הלכה א'.
110. אורח חיים, סימן תקפ"ט, סעיף ו'.
111. מטה אפרים, סימן תקפ"ט, סעיף ד', משנה ברורה, סימן תקפ"ז, ס"ק ט"ז.
112. חיי אדם, כלל קמ"א, ס"ק ז'.
113. שו"ת שאגת אריה, סימן ק"ח, שערי תשובה, סימן תקפ"ט, ד"ה "אע"פ".
114. שו"ת יוסף אומץ להחיד"א, סימן פ"ב.
115. מטה אפרים, סימן תקפ"ט, סעיף ד', משנה ברורה, סימן תקפ"ז, ס"ק ט"ז.
116. משנה תורה, הלכות שביתת עשור, פרק א', הלכה ד'.
117. אורח חיים, סימן תרט"ז, סעיפים א', ב'.
118. שם, סעיף ב', משנה ברורה שם, ס"ק י"ד.
119. משנה ברורה שם, ס"ק ג'.
120. כף החיים שם, ס"ק ט'.
121. אורח חיים שם, סעיף ב'.
122. משנה ברורה שם, ס"ק ו'.
123. שו"ת עשה לך רב, חלק ו', סימן מ"ד.
124. אורח חיים, סימן תרט"ז, סעיף ב', משנה ברורה שם, ס"ק ו'.
125. רמ"א שם.
126. ב"ח שם, מגן אברהם שם, ס"ק ב'.
127. חיי אדם, כלל ס"ו, סעיף י"א.
128. שולחן ערוך הגרש"ז, סימן תרט"ז, סעיף י"א, משנה ברורה שם, ס"ק ט', ערוך השולחן שם, סעיף ז'.
129. אורח חיים, סימן תרי"ג.
130. שם, סימן תרי"ד, סעיף א'.
131. שם, סעיף ב'.
132. אורח חיים, סימן תרט"ז, סעיף א', מגן אברהם שם, ס"ק א', משנה ברורה שם, ס"ק ג'.
133. שולחן ערוך הגרש"ז, סימן תרט"ז, ס"ק ב', ג', ד'.
134. אורח חיים, סימן תרי"ג, סעיף א'.
135. אורחות חיים, סימן תרי"ח, ס"ק י"ב.
136. אורח חיים, סימן תרל"ט, סעיפים א', ב'.
137. אורח חיים, סימן תר"מ, סעיף א', משנה ברורה שם, ס"ק א'.
138. אורח חיים שם, סעיף ב'.
139. מגן אברהם שם, ס"ק ב'.
140. ב"ח שם, אליה רבה שם, ס"ק ג'.

141. חיי אדם, כלל קמ"ג, סעיף כ"ה, שולחן ערוך הגרש"ז, סימן תר"מ, סעיף ג', ערוך השולחן שם, סעיף ב'.
142. משנה ברורה, סימן תר"מ, ס"ק ד'.
143. ערוך השולחן שם, סעיף ב'.
144. משנה תורה, הלכות לולב, פרק ז', הלכה י"ט.
145. סוכה, דף מ"ב, עמוד א'.
146. אורח חיים, סימן תרנ"ז.
147. פרי מגדים, משבצות זהב שם, ס"ק א', משנה ברורה שם, ס"ק א'.
148. מגן אברהם שם, ס"ק א', פרי מגדים, אשל אברהם שם.
149. ט"ז שם, ס"ק א'.
150. שם.
151. פרי מגדים, משבצות זהב שם, ס"ק א', משנה ברורה שם, ס"ק ד', דרך החיים, סדר נטילת לולב.
152. שו"ת אגרות משה, אורח חיים, חלק ג', סימן צ"ה.
153. ביאור הלכה, סימן תרנ"ז, ד"ה "כדי לחנכם".
154. ביאור הלכה, סימן תרע"ה, סעיף ג', ד"ה "ולדידן".
155. אורח חיים, סימן תרנ"ח, סעיף א'.
156. שם, סעיפים ג', ד'.
157. שם, סעיף ו'.
158. פרי מגדים, אשל אברהם, סימן תרנ"ח, ס"ק ח', משנה ברורה שם, ס"ק כ"ג.
159. בגדי ישע שם, ס"ק ח', ברכי יוסף שם, ס"ק ו'.
160. מגן אברהם שם, ס"ק ח', פרי מגדים, אשל אברהם שם, חיי אדם כלל קנ"ג, סעיף י"א.
161. ביכורי יעקב, סימן תרנ"ח, ס"ק י"ח.
162. שו"ת אגרות משה, חלק ג', סימן צ"ה.
163. אורח חיים, סימן תרס"ט, ברמ"א, משנה ברורה שם, ס"ק י"ב.
164. שם.
165. שערי אפרים, שער ח', סעיף נ"ז, כף החיים, סימן תרס"ד, ס"ק ד'.
166. משנה ברורה, סימן תרס"ט, ס"ק י"ד.
167. מגן אברהם, סימן תרע"א, ס"ק א', משנה ברורה שם, ס"ק ד'.
168. אורח חיים, סימן תרע"א, סעיף ב'.
169. באר היטב שם, ס"ק ג'.
170. מגן אברהם, סימן תרע"ז, ס"ק ח', פרי מגדים, אשל אברהם שם.
171. אורח חיים, סימן תרע"ה, סעיף ג', ברמ"א.
172. מגן אברהם, סימן תרע"ז, ס"ק ח', פרי מגדים, אשל אברהם שם.
173. ביאור הלכה, סימן תרע"ה, ד"ה "ולדידן".
174. חיי אדם, כלל קנ"ד, סעיף ז', ליקוטי מהרי"ח, דיני ומנהגי חנוכה.
175. אליה רבה, סימן תרע"א, ס"ק ג', שערים המצויינים בהלכה, סימן קל"ט, ס"ק י'.
176. אורח חיים, סימן תרפ"ט, סעיף א'.
177. אורח חיים, סימן תרפ"ז, סעיף א'.

178. אורח חיים, סימן תרפ"ט, סעיף א'.
179. משנה ברורה שם, ס"ק ג'.
180. מגן אברהם שם, ס"ק י"א, ביאור הלכה שם, ד"ה „מנהג טוב".
181. משנה ברורה שם, ס"ק י"ח.
182. אורח חיים, סימן תרצ"ה, סעיף ד', ברמ"א, משנה ברורה שם, ס"ק כ"ה.
183. פרי מגדים, אשל אברהם שם, ס"ק י"ד.
184. אורח חיים, סימן תרצ"ד, סעיף א' ברמ"א.
185. לבוש החור, סימן תרפ"ו, סעיף ב', אליה רבה שם, ס"ק ב'.
186. מגן אברהם, סימן תרצ"ד, ס"ק ג'.
187. חיי אדם, כלל קנ"ה, סעיף ד', ערוך השולחן, סימן תרצ"ד, סעיף ח'.
188. מגן אברהם, סימן תרצ"ד, ס"ק ג', משנה ברורה שם, ס"ק ה'.
189. מסכת פסחים, דף ק"ח, עמוד ב', דף ק"ט, עמוד א'.
190. אורח חיים, סימן תקכ"ט, סעיף ב'.
191. שם, סימן תקל"א, סימן תקל"ד.
192. שם, סימן תקל"א, סעיף ו'.
193. מגן אברהם, שם, ס"ק ח'.
194. משנה ברורה שם, ס"ק ט"ו.
195. אורח חיים, סימן תקל"ד, סעיף א'.
196. שם ברמ"א, משנה ברורה שם, ס"ק י"א.
197. שמירת שבת כהלכתה, מהדורא קמא, פרק כ"ט, סעיפים מ"ח, מ"ט.

Chapter Five

Chinuch for General Mitzvot

The life of a Jew is governed by his adherence to a general framework of prohibitions and positive duties. These mitzvot are not connected with the daily regimen of life or specific holidays of the year. They apply constantly throughout one's life or at special periods of one's existence. It is these mitzvot which in a sense really define a person's identity as a Torah-observant Jew. The obligation of chinuch, of course, applies to these duties as it does to all other mitzvot. This chapter covers the responsibility of parents in training their children to observe these prohibitions and positive obligations.

Kashruth: Non-Kosher Medicine

The laws of kashruth are certainly among the central mitzvot which define an observant Jewish lifestyle. Observance of these laws serves in many ways as the cornerstone of a person's religious life. The duty of chinuch obligates parents to stop their children from consuming non-kosher food, once the child has achieved the maturity of being able to understand that such food is forbidden. Children below that age do not have to be stopped from eating these foods if they take them themselves.[1] This is true from a strict halachic perspective. However, the poskim advise that parents should not permit their children to consume non-kosher food even from the time of birth. Allowing a very young child to eat non-kosher food is not forbidden, but consumption of these foods has a corrupting influence on the child's subsequent spiritual growth. Parents, therefore, should attempt to stop such behavior.[2] Under all circumstances parents are forbidden to physically give any non-kosher food to a child from the time of the child's birth. In this case, they would be actively causing their child to sin.³ Most poskim do not differentiate between food which is rabbinically non-kosher and that which is non-kosher by Torah law. In both cases parents are not permitted to give such items to their children.⁴ Some Rishonim argue that parents may feed non-kosher food to children if they require such food, as long as the items in question are only rabbinically forbidden, but that there is no such permissibility for things which are non-kosher by Torah law.⁵ This, however, remains the minority opinion. The generally accepted prinicple is that parents may not feed even rabbinically prohibited foods to children.⁶

The laws of kashruth usually do not present any problem for parents. This is not so, however, when a sick child requires food or medication which is non-kosher. There is no doubt that if the illness is potentially life-threatening any medication may be used. The laws of kashruth are cancelled even for adults in this type of situation.⁷ The correct course of action is less clear when the illness does not present a danger to life. Here the issue is whether a parent is permitted to give trefah items to his child in order to effect a cure, thereby violating his responsibility of chinuch to the child.

Magen Avraham recommends that in such a case the parent ask a non-Jew to give the trefah food or medicine to the child. This is permissible because Torah law only forbids directly feeding trefah items to the child. Thus, when the parent asks a non-Jew to do this, he merely violates the rabbinic prohibition against using a gentile to perform a prohibited act. The rabbinic decree does not apply in any case of illness.⁸ If a non-Jew is unavailable, *Magen Avraham* indicates that the parent may himself give the food or medicine to the child if the forbidden item is only rabbinically prohibited. However, if the object in question is prohibited by Torah law, no such permissibility exists. Then the medicine must be administered by a non-Jew, or the child must be told to take it himself.⁹ *Siftei Kohen* argues that even when the medicine is only rabbinically prohibited it may not be given to the child by the parent. A parent may only do this in the case of a life-threatening disease.[10] Some poskim agree with this more restrictive position.[11] Others decide in accordance with *Magen Avraham*.[12] It would seem that in case of necessity parents may follow the more lenient approach.[13] *Magen Avraham* further rules that if a non-Jew is unavailable the parent is permitted to tell a Jewish minor to give the trefah medicine to the sick child. Here again, the parent by doing this is only violating a rabbinic prohibition. This decree does not apply in a case of illness.[14] *Magen Avraham's* suggestion is accepted by later poskim.[15]

Kashruth: Milk and Meat

The prohibition against eating meat cooked together with milk is one of the most distinctive laws of kashruth. Torah law prohibits the consumption of these two items only when cooked together. However, by rabbinic decree it is forbidden to eat meat and milk in any type of combination.[16] The rabbis further prohibited the consumption of milk after the eating of meat even when the two are eaten separately.[17] There is a debate among the Rishonim as to how much time must elapse between the consumption of meat and milk. Many authorities state that it is necessary to wait a period of six hours between meat and milk. Others say that a lesser amount of time is sufficient.[18] Rabbi Yosef Caro decides in the *Shulchan Aruch* that a wait of six hours is necessary. Rema notes that the Ashkenazic practice is to consume milk one hour after eating meat, but he too recommends a six-hour wait as the correct course of action.[19] The later poskim generally accept six hours as the necessary time to wait in order to drink milk after eating meat.[20] In certain Western European Jewish communities, however, the popular practice continues to follow the minhag quoted by Rema or some variation of it.[21]

This law often causes a problem for parents of infants and toddlers. The requirements of chinuch prohibit parents from giving forbidden food to children from the time of birth. During the first year or two of life, babies are generally given a bottle of formula or milk soon after they have completed their meal. This is done even when the meal included meat foods. It is usually very impractical to separate the bottle from the meal or to give the milk before the solid food. When a child is breast-feeding this is not a problem, since one is permitted to consume human milk immediately after eating meat.[22] However, once the child is changed to cow's milk this question becomes an issue relevant to all babies.

The best solution to the problem is for parents to wait at least one hour after meat before giving milk to their baby. In this way, they satisfy the Halachah according to the practice quoted by Rema. The poskim state that it is acceptable to rely on this opinion in the case of a child or even an adult who is slightly ill.[23] This generally can be easily done sometime in the child's second year. It may, however, pose great difficulties with a younger baby. In that case, parents who must give milk to their child within an hour after meat rely on the opinion of those Rishonim who permit the violation of a rabbinic law for the benefit of a child. As mentioned earlier, this view is not accepted by many poskim under normal circumstances. All authorities, however, agree that in a case of real necessity parents may follow this opinion.[24] There is an additional reason for allowing this practice when necessary. Some authorities permit parents to cause a child to violate any rabbinic law as long as the law in question is only a gezerah, a preventive decree, rather than an independent prohibiton on its own.[25] The prohibition on consuming milk after meat would seem to fall into this category. It is obvious that once children are capable of waiting one hour after meat before receiving milk parents are obligated to make sure that they do so. It is similarly clear that once children reach kindergarten age parents are required to teach them to wait a full six hours after eating meat, or whatever the accepted practice of waiting is in their community. Some poskim argue that a child under nine years old who strongly demands milk and will not drink anything else in its place may be given milk an hour after a meat meal. Once the child is older, however, this is no longer permitted.[26]

Dolls and Magic

Halachah contains many prohibitions associated with the Torah's ban on idolatry. It is not only forbidden to worship idols but also to have any connection with things that resemble idols. In this connection a Jew is forbidden to own a graven image, even when it is not worshipped as an idol. A statue of a human being, depicted in full with all his limbs, is included in the prohibition. One is only permitted to own such items when the image of the human is woven or painted so that it does not protrude or when only a part of the body is depicted.[27] Statues or images of animals are not included in the prohibition.[28]

This law presents a problem for parents in regard to human dolls. Children desire such toys, and parents would find it very difficult to deny them these playthings. However, dolls are usually made as full images of the human body and should therefore be included in the prohibition of owning a graven image. Of course, no such problem exists in regard to animal dolls.

There are halachic grounds which permit parents to buy human dolls for their children. Later poskim point out that under contemporary conditions it is permitted to own statues which depict the full human body. They argue that the reason for the original prohibition was that when a Jew owned such an object it might appear as if he worshipped it as an idol. Since nowadays it is clear that this is not the case with ordinary statues, the prohibition no longer applies to them.[29] This argument certainly holds true for dolls. Other authorities state further that only a statue made to last permanently and kept in a safe place is forbidden, for only in such a case does the statue appear to be an idol. Dolls and similar toys are expected to break and not kept in a secure place in the home, and therefore are not included in the prohibition.[30] Later poskim have accepted these arguments and regard human dolls as totally permitted.[31]

Another prohibition connected with idolatory relates to the

Chinuch for General Mitzvot

performance of magic acts or shows. All such activities are forbidden, whether done by charms and incantations or by trickery and sleight of hand.[32] In the latter case no idolatry is involved, but the prohibition remains the same.[33] *Chochmat Adam* points out that while the main prohibition here is on performing acts of magic, it is also forbidden to view magic shows or performances. Someone who attends a magic show aids and abets the commission of a prohibited activity.[34] Children generally enjoy magic acts and shows and often wish to attend them. Parents, as part of their duty of chinuch, would seem to be required to stop them from doing so.

There is, however, one case where parents may allow children to attend such shows. Since it is not a sin for a non-Jew to put on a magic act, many poskim hold that there is no restriction on taking children to see a magic show with non-Jewish performers.[35] In addition some poskim argue that there is no prohibition on performing magic acts or attending magic shows when the performer makes it clear that his performance is being done by natural rather than supernatural means. These types of shows would then be permitted even with Jewish performers.[36] Many other authorities, however, state that magic acts of any type may not be attended when presented by Jewish performers.[37]

Haircutting and Clothing

A Jew is restricted by Halachah in the manner in which he may cut his hair. The Torah identifies five areas on the face and head known as *peot*. Three of these *peot* may not be removed by a razor. They may, however, be cut closely with a scissors or a device similar to a scissors. Since the exact location of the *peot* is unclear, the poskim state that it is proper to avoid using a razor on any part of the beard.[38] The two other peot are located at the two temples of the head. The *Shulcahn Aruch* states that the peot may not be cut with scissors even when the cutting makes the skin clean of all hair as if it were done with a razor. They may, however, be trimmed and cropped.[39] These laws apply only to males and not to females.[40]

Obviously the prohibition on cutting the peot of the beard is not relevant to minor boys, because they have no facial hair in those areas. By contrast, the restrictions on the peot of the head do apply to them. It is forbidden for an adult to shave these areas of a boy's head, just as it is prohibited to do so to the head of another adult.[41] This issue becomes relevant when contemporary barbers use a razor or a very close hair clipper to clean the area around the ears of all hair. According to many opinions these areas are included in the peot of the head. While they may be trimmed, they may not have all traces of hair removed as if shaved with a razor.[42] Even if the barber is a non-Jew this prohibition remains in effect. Parents are required by the duty of chinuch to see to it that their sons do not violate the Torah prohibitions involved in this type of action.[43] Since these laws do not apply to women, there are no restrictions on haircutting for minor girls.

From the standpoint of Halachah there is no prescribed time at which a child's hair should first be cut and no specified manner in which it should be done. A custom exists in some communities of not cutting a boy's hair until he reaches the age of three. At that time a celebration is held and the boy's hair is cut, leaving the peot of the head intact.[44] This practice is not followed in many other communities.

A Jew is prohibited from wearing clothing meant for the opposite sex and from making his bodily appearance resemble that of the opposite sex. Jewelry, styles of haircutting, and accessories of various types are all included in this prohibition. If any of these things are exclusively used by either males or females, members of the other sex may not adopt them.[45] This prohibition applies even when the article in question has the same pattern for men and women but is made in different colors for each sex.[46]

Parents are bound by the duty of chinuch to see to it that their children observe this prohibition. Even when children are below the age of understanding, parents may not dress them in clothes or styles of the opposite sex. By doing so, the parent would be actively causing their child to sin. This is prohibited from the time of a child's birth.[47] The specific place and time in which a person lives are the factors which determine what is to be considered a feminine or masculine garment or style.[48] A common example of how this prohibition applies is provided by baby or toddler clothes. These garments are often identical in style and pattern for boys and girls but different in color. If a certain color is customarily designated as appropriate for babies of one sex, parents would be forbidden to use garments of that color for children of the opposite sex.

Another restriction on clothing is the law of shatnez. A Jew is forbidden to wear or use clothing or textiles made of a combination of wool and linen.[49] Parents are bound by the duty of chinuch to ensure that their children do not violate this prohibition. They may not place shatnez clothing or coverings on infants from the time of their birth, for by doing so they would actively be causing their child to sin.[50]

Vows

The Torah does not encourage the making of vows or oaths even for creditable purposes. However, if an adult Jew does make a vow he is required to abide by it, unless he has it anulled in the proper manner. Normally children below the age of bar mitzvah or bat mitzvah are not personally obligated to fulfill mitzvot. Parents are rquired to train children to observe mitzvot as a fulfillment of the parental duty of chinuch. The child himself has no such obligation. Vows are an exception to this rule. Children within one year of adulthood (boys over twelve and girls over eleven) are, under certain conditions, personally required to fulfill vows which they have made, just as adults must. In such cases the intellectual maturity of the vow-maker must be tested. If the child understands the concept of making an oath and the responsibility such an act entails, he or she is required to abide by the words of the vow exactly as an adult must.[51] The examination of intellectual maturity must be made at the time of the oath. We do not rely on the results of a test given earlier.[52]

Children more than a year below the age of adulthood are not bound by oaths which they make even if they are mature enough to understand the meaning of what they are doing. Nevertheless, parents should make sure that their child fulfills his oath if the vow concerns only a minor matter which does not involve much self-deprivation. This should be done so that the child is educated to understand the binding importance of vows and oaths. If the oath is too burdensome for a young child to fulfill, parents do not have to force the child to abide by it. They should, however, punish the child appropriately for making such a vow. This is done, again, to teach the child the serious nature of a vow from the perspective of Halachah.[53]

Death and Mourning

Halachah has many requirements for a Jew who suffers the death of a close relative. These obligations begin from the moment of death and continue for the year of mourning in different forms. It is obvious that minor children can also suffer the loss of close relatives. The requirements of mourning for minors are, however, quite different from those for adults.

The first obligation of a Jew, whether a male or female, who has lost a close relative is to tear *keriah*, that is, to rend his garment. This was originally performed at the time of death but is commonly done today in conjunction with the funeral service.[54] The Talmud states that a minor in such a case should have keriah done on his garment just as it would be done for an adult.[55] The *Shulchan Aruch* codifies this as binding halachah.[56] *Turei Zahav* argues that this is proof that parents should ensure that minor children observe all the obligations of mourning as a fulfillment of their responsibility of chinuch.[57] *Siftei Kohen* disagrees. He states that such a requirement only exists for keriah but not for any other law of mourning.[58] Many later authorities agree with this position.[59] There are some, however, who argue that *Turei Zahav* is correct and a minor should observe all the laws of mourning with the possible exception of the restriction of studying Torah during shivah.[60] The contemporary practice is not to obligate minors below the age of bar mitzvah or bat mitzvah to fulfill any of the requirements of mourning except for keriah. This exemption includes both the obligation of shivah and those of the later year of mourning.[61]

Someone who attains the age of bar mitzvah or bat mitzvah during the week of shivah is not required to observe the laws of mourning for the remainder of the shivah period. He or she was not obligated to follow these laws when shivah began, due to being a minor, and therefore is not required to observe them after becoming an adult. Since the period of mourning is regarded as a complete unit, one is not obligated to observe it in a partial form.[62] Despite this, *Chochmat Adam* states that a minor who reaches adulthood during the twelve months of mourning should observe the requisite restrictions. He argues that the prohibitions of the twelve-month period are not the result of mourning but rather of the requirement to honor parents which the orphan is obligated to fulfill.[63]

There is an additional prohibition associated with death and mourning which applies to minors. A kohen is forbidden to have physical contact with a dead body or to be under one roof with a corpse. This prohibition applies only to male kohanim and not to females.[64] Parents of kohanim are required by the mitzvah of chinuch to see to it that their minor sons do not violate these prohibitions. They must stop their sons from coming into contact with the dead in any manner forbidden to adult kohanim. There is no such obligation for daughters of kohanim, for as adult women none of these restrictions will apply to them. This requirement begins when a boy reaches the age of understanding, as it does with all mitzvot. Even before that point parents of kohanim may not actively bring their sons into contact with the dead. This is prohibited from the time of the child's birth.[65]

This requirement of chinuch extends to a case where the minor son of a kohen is asleep in a house in which someone has died. The parents are required to wake the boy and remove him from the premises. This is because every minute the boy remains in the house with the corpse he is violating the laws of purity for a kohen. His parents are obligated by the responsibility of chinuch to prevent this.[66] However, if the child in question is below the age of understanding this no longer holds. The obligation of chinuch does not apply to a child so young. His parents may not bring him into such a house, but if he entered it prior to the occurrence of death they need not remove him from it.[67]

The pregnant wife of a kohen may enter a house containing a corpse. This is permitted even though she is actively bringing her future child, who may be a male kohen, into forbidden premises. There are two reasons for allowing this. In the first instance it is unclear whether or not she is carrying a viable male fetus. Secondly, the fetus is enclsoed in the womb and totally separated from the impurities of the outside world.[68]

Adult kohanim are permitted to come into contact with the dead when the deceased is a close relative. Indeed, in such cases they are required to attend to the needs of the dead despite their priestly status.[69] Some poskim argue that this is not true in regard to minor kohanim. Parents are bound by the duty of chinuch to prevent children from defiling themselves even for close relatives. The rationale is that since minors are not obligated by the duty of chinuch to observe the laws of mourning, they have no reason to attend to the needs of the dead.[70] Other authorities disagree. They say that a minor kohen cannot have stricter obligations than an adult. Since an adult may defile himself for a close relative, a minor may do so as well.[71] Many later poskim state that while it is preferable for a minor not to defile himself for close relatives, parents are not requried to stop him from doing so on his own. In such a case they may rely on the lenient opinion.[72]

Yichud

It is forbidden by Jewish law for a member of one sex to be alone with a member of the opposite sex for more than a minimal amount of time in a place which is inaccessible to the public. This is due to the fear of something immoral happening.[73] When additional people, other than the two individuals of the opposite sex, are present the law changes. In a normal urban situation two men are allowed to be alone with one woman, since each of the men serves as a chaperone for the other. In an isolated area three men are necessary.[74] Rema similarly permits three women to be alone with one man since the women serve as chaperones for each other. However, two women cannot serve as guardians for one another. Three are necessary.[75] Other poskim do not accept this latter leniency.[76] When the individuals are not in a locked, inaccessible area there is no prohibition of yichud at all.[77]

The laws of chinuch make parents responsible for ensuring that their children observe the prohibitions of yichud. None of the yichud laws apply to children who are too young for any sexual misconduct to take place. Halachah defines this as three years of age for girls and nine years of age for boys. Children younger than this may be left with members of the opposite sex under all circumstances. Once children reach these ages, however, the laws of yichud apply fully to them.[78] Despite this, a boy and a girl who have not attained the ages of bar mitzvah and bat mitzvah may be left alone together. Boys above the age of nine and girls older than three are forbidden to be left alone with members of the opposite sex only when the others are halachically adults. This means that they are above bar mitzvah or bat mitzvah age. If both individuals being left alone together are halachically considered to be children, no prohibition of yichud exists.[79]

There is no prohibition of yichud when a son is left with a mother, a daughter with a father, or a brother with a sister. This is true even if one of the individuals in each of these pairs is an adult and the other is a child above the age of nine or three or also an adult.[80] This enables normal family life to continue undisturbed with parents or siblings of one sex being alone with children or siblings of the opposite sex. Similarly there is no prohibition of yichud for a grandparent with a grandchild of the opposite sex.[81] This is, however, only true for blood relatives. Step-parents and step-grandparents do fall within the category of those covered by the laws of yichud. They are prohibited from being alone with children or grandchildren of the opposite sex who are above the ages of three or nine respectively. Of course, when the child's natural parent is present, no such prohibition applies.

The prohibition of yichud only applies when two individuals are in an inaccessible place. The *Shulchan Aruch* states that if the door is open there is no prohibition of yichud.[82] Poskim disagree as to whether a closed door which is unlocked will fall into this category and remove the prohibition of yichud. Many contemporary authorities follow this lenient opinion.[83] Those who follow this view also allow yichud in a locked house when someone on the outside has a key and can enter at any time.[84] These leniencies seem to be applicable in the case of a babysitter who is with a child of the opposite sex when the child is above the age of three or nine respectively. Since the parents have the key and can return at any time, there are grounds for permitting this type of situation.

Tziniut

In contemporary society it is regarded as completely appropriate for open displays of affection to take place between members of the opposite sexes. Actions such as hugging or kissing are considered to be no more than friendly gestures between relatives or even strangers. This is certainly true in regard to children. Older relatives or friends of the family think nothing of kissing or embracing the children of friends or relatives.

The attitude of Halachah is very different. Jewish law prescribes that open displays of affection between the sexes must be restricted to husbands and wives or parents and children. This is part of proper *tziniut*, or modest behavior. Other individuals, whether relatives or strangers, must refrain from these actions.[85] Grandparents are in the category of parents and permitted to display affection to their grandchildren of the opposite sex.[86] Some poskim also permit older brothers to be affectionate with their sisters.[87]

This prohibition applies to both adults and children. One may not kiss or embrace a child of the opposite sex, unless that child is one's own or one's grandchild.[88] There is no such restriction for a child who is below the age of possible sexual misconduct. Halachah defines this age as nine for boys and three for girls, as noted above.[89] Thus there is no problem with displays of affectionate behavior towards infants or toddlers, no matter what their personal status may be. However, once children reach the age of three or nine such activities cannot be condoned.

Another facet of life governed by the concept of tziniut concerns the matter of proper clothing. It is considered indecent behavior for a woman to expose certain areas of her body in public. The *Shulchan Aruch* states that one may not recite the Shema in the presence of a woman who has exposed one *tefach*, or handbreadth, of a part of her body which is normally covered in public. This is because the Shema may not be said in the presence of indecent exposure.[90] The later poskim explain that in cultures where it is acceptable for women to uncover their faces, hands, or feet, those areas are not required to be covered. However, the arm above the elbow and the leg above the knee must always be clothed in public even when the prevailing pattern is to leave these areas uncovered as well. These latter parts of the body remain forbidden under all circumstances.[91] This means that a Jewish woman is required by Halachah to keep her arms above the elbow and her legs above the knee covered in public at all times. Not doing this is considered a violation of good moral behavior and may even be grounds for divorce.[92] No such restrictions exist for a man. He may uncover all parts of his body as longs as no actual indecent exposure takes place.[93]

Parents are faced with the problem of properly clothing their minor sons and daughters. Since no restrictions exist for a man's clothing, it is obvious that no prohibitions exist for minor boys either. However, there is a question as to what constitutes acceptable clothing for minor girls. The Chofetz Chaim argues that a girl above the age of three is equal to an adult woman in this respect. Since from that age a girl is considered liable to be the object of sexual misconduct she must be treated as an adult. This means that her arms above the elbow and her legs above the knee must be covered in public.[94] This obviously presents difficulties for the parents of girls under the age of elementary school in choosing proper clothes for their daughters. The Chazon Ish disagrees. He states that for such young children these areas of the body cannot be considered indecent. As long as the girl has not matured sufficiently there is no need to consider these body parts as forbidden. There is no uniform age at which the need to cover them begins. It depends on the dimensions and maturity of each girl's body.[95] Other authorities agree with this lenient opinion.[96]

The laws of tziniut forbid excessively close affectionate behavior, such as sleeping together in one bed with body parts touching, even for parents and older children of the opposite sex. Once children are bar mitzvah or bat mitzvah there is no doubt that such behavior is prohibited. However, even before that point parents should avoid these actions. The time when such behavior is forbidden begins with the physical and emotional maturity of the individual child. Once minors have reached a point where they are embarrased to be seen unclothed by a parent of the opposite sex these actions become forbidden. It is obvious that when a child has reached such a point of development the parents should no longer dress the child or allow themselves to see their son or daughter in an unclothed state. Normally this point is reached long before the age of bar mitzvah or bat mitzvah. Of course, before this point is reached no such restrictions exist.[97]

The rules for a parent taking a child of the opposite sex swimming fall into the same category. It is prohibited by Halachah for members of the opposite sex to swim together, because women's bathing suits reveal parts of the body which must be covered in public.[98] Once a girl has reached the point where she is embarrased to be seen unclothed by her father, he may no longer take her swimming with him. This age, of course, will depend on her physical and intellectual maturity.[99] When other males, in addition to the father, are present the situation is different. The girl, in this case, is dressed in a bathing suit, which clearly reveals parts of the body normally required to be covered in the presence of men. If we follow the opinion of the Chofetz Chaim, quoted earlier, it is forbidden for her to do this from the age of three.[100] However, if we follow the more lenient view of the Chazon Ish, this only becomes prohibited when a girl has matured sufficiently to become attractive to members of the opposite sex. This will depend on the physical dimensions and maturity of the body of each individual girl. Until that point is reached no prohibition would exist.[101]

Similarly, a mother may take her minor son swimming with her until the point where she is ashamed to be unclothed in his presence. Once the boy has reached such a stage of development this becomes forbidden. This age, again, depends on the individual situation.[102] When other women are present in bathing suits the situation changes. Since a male adult is forbidden to gaze at women in such a state, the duty of chinuch obligates parents to restrain a boy who has reached the age of understanding from violating this prohibition.

The concept of tziniut extends to hearing women sing. Males are forbidden to listen to a woman singing, since this might lead to suggestive thoughts on the part of certain individuals. The prohibition applies to all adult women in contemporary times.[103] Rabbi Moshe Feinstein states that once a girl reaches the age of eleven it becomes forbidden to listen to her singing voice, just as one may not listen to the song of an adult woman. This is based on the girl's having reached physical maturity by that time. Before that age, however, a male may listen to a girl singing when it is necessary for him to do so.[104] This argument allows schools and other institutions to present vocal performances involving their female students up to the age of eleven. Rabbi Yechiel Weinberg writes that these activities are permitted even with older girls. He gives two reasons for this. In the first place there is no prohibition against hearing the voices of more than one person. What is forbidden by Halachah is a single female singing voice. This would mean that a choral performance with no female solosit would be permitted. In addition, he argues, when the purpose of such singing is not immoral but to achieve a religious or educational goal, there is no prohibition on males listening to such songs. This would provide an even broader leniency for such performances.[105]

One last point involving tziniut concerns marital relations. Halachah specifies that husband and wife may not engage in such relations in the presence of other people. This is true even if the others are asleep. It is, however, permissible to have relations in a room where an infant is present. Once the infant is old enough to be able to speak, this becomes forbidden. In such a case, the child must be moved to a different room or a divider must be placed in front of the child to make sure that he remains unaware of what is occurring.[106]

Notes

1. אורח חיים, סימן שמ"ג, מגן אברהם שם, ס"ק ב'.
2. יורה דעה, סימן פ"א, סעיף ז' ברמ"א, ש"ך שם, ס"ק כ"ו.
3. אורח חיים, סימן שמ"ג, מגן אברהם שם, ס"ק ב'.
4. מגן אברהם שם, משנה ברורה שם, ס"ק ג'.
5. שו"ת רשב"א חלק א', סימן צ"ב, פירוש הר"ן, ריש מסכת יומא.
6. ש"ך יורה דעה סימן פ"א, ס"ק כ"א, חיי אדם, כלל ס"ו, סעיף ו'.
7. יורה דעה, סימן קנ"ז, סעיף א'.
8. מגן אברהם, סימן שמ"ג, ס"ק ג'.
9. שם.
10. ש"ך, יורה דעה, סימן פ"א, ס"ק כ"א.

11. פרי חדש שם, ס"ק כ"א, כריתי שם, ס"ק י"ד.
12. גליון מהרש"א שם על הש"ך, שולחן ערוך הגרש"ז, אורח חיים, סימן שמ"ג, סעיף ו'.
13. כף החיים, יורה דעה, סימן פ"א, ס"ק נ"ח.
14. מגן אברהם, סימן שמ"ג, ס"ק ג'.
15. משנה ברורה שם, ס"ק ה'.
16. יורה דעה, סימן פ"ז, סעיף א'.
17. יורה דעה, סימן פ"ט, סעיף א'.
18. טור, יורה דעה, סימן פ"ט, דרכי משה שם, ס"ק ה'.
19. יורה דעה, סימן פ"ט, סעיף א'.
20. פרי מגדים שם, שפתי דעת ס"ק ה', חכמת אדם כלל מ', ס"ק י"ג.
21. See Isidor Grunfeld, *The Jewish Dietary Laws* (London: Soncino Press, 1972), pp. 24–25.
22. כף החיים, יורה דעה, סימן פ"ז, ס"ק כ"ט.
23. חכמת אדם, כלל מ', ס"ק י"ג, ערוך השולחן, יורה דעה, סימן פ"ט, סעיף ז'.
24. מגן אברהם, סימן שמ"ג, ס"ק ג', שולחן ערוך הגרש"ז, שם, סעיף ו', חיי אדם, כלל ס"ו, סעיף ו'.
25. דעת תורה, אורח חיים, סימן שמ"ג, ד"ה „ואפילו בדברים האסורים משום שבות".
26. שו"ת חלקת יעקב, חלק ב', סימן פ"ח.
27. יורה דעה, סימן קמ"א, סעיף ד', ש"ך שם, ס"ק כ"ה.
28. שם, סעיף ו', ש"ך שם, ס"ק ל"א.
29. חכמת אדם, כלל פ"ה, סעיף ו'.
30. שו"ת מהרי"ט, חלק ב', סימן ל"ה.
31. שו"ת יחוה דעת, חלק ג', סימן ס"ד.
32. יורה דעה, סימן קע"ט, סעיף ט"ו.
33. ש"ך שם, ס"ק י"ז.
34. חכמת אדם, כלל פ"ט, סעיף ו'.
35. חכמת אדם שם, דרכי תשובה, סימן קע"ט, ס"ק ל"ז.
36. שו"ת עשה לך רב, חלק א', סימן מ"ד.
37. חכמת אדם, כלל פ"ט, סעיף ו'.
38. דרכי תשובה, For a discussion of the exact dimensions of the head *peot*, see סימן קפ"א, ס"ק י"ג
39. יורה דעה, סימן קפ"א, סעיפים א', ג', ש"ך שם, ס"ק ב'.
40. יורה דעה שם, סעיפים ו', י"ג.
41. יורה דעה שם, סעיף ה'.
42. דרכי תשובה, סימן קפ"א, ס"ק י"ג.
43. פתחי תשובה שם, ס"ק ג'.
44. שערי תשובה, אורח חיים, סימן תקל"א, ס"ק ז'.
45. יורה דעה, סימן קפ"ב.
46. חכמת אדם, כלל צ', ס"ק א'.

47. שו"ת מנחת יצחק, חלק ג', סימן ק"ח.
48. יורה דעה, סימן קפ"ב, סעיף ה'.
49. יורה דעה, סימן רצ"ח.
50. ברכי יוסף, אורח חיים, סימן שמ"ג, ס"ק ו'.
51. יורה דעה, סימן רל"ג, סעיף א'.
52. ש"ך שם, ס"ק א'.
53. רמ"א שם, סעיף א'.
54. כל בו על אבילות, פרק א', סימן ב', קריעה ס"ק ג'.
55. מועד קטן, דף כ"ו, עמוד ב'.
56. יורה דעה, סימן ש"מ, סעיף כ"ז.
57. ט"ז שם, ס"ק ט"ו.
58. נקודת הכסף שם, ד"ה „מכאן ראייה".
59. דגול מרבבה שם, ד"ה „צריך לנהוג", חכמת אדם, כלל קנ"ב, סעיף י"ז.
60. כל בו על אבילות, פרק ד', סימן א', ס"ק כ"ח.
61. שו"ת אגרות משה, יורה דעה, חלק א', סימן רכ"ד, גשר החיים, חלק א', פרק י"ט, סימן ג', ס"ק ב'.
62. יורה דעה, סימן שצ"ו, סעיף ג', ט"ז שם, ס"ק ב'.
63. חכמת אדם, כלל קס"ח, סעיף ו'.
64. משנה תורה, הלכות אבל, פרק ג', הלכות א', י"א, יורה דעה, סימן שס"ט.
65. יורה דעה, סימן שע"ג, סעיף א', ט"ז שם, ס"ק א', ש"ך שם, ס"ק א'.
66. ט"ז שם, ס"ק א', ש"ך שם, ס"ק א'.
67. בית הלל, סימן שע"א, בהגהה שם, פתחי תשובה שם, ס"ק א'.
68. ש"ך, יורה דעה, סימן שע"א, ס"ק א'.
69. יורה דעה, סימן שע"ג, סעיף ג'.
70. פתחי תשובה, שם, ס"ק א'.
71. שו"ת אחיעזר, חלק ג', סימן פ"א, ס"ק ו'.
72. גשר החיים, חלק א', פרק ו', סימן ה', ס"ק י', כל בו על אבילות, פרק א', סימן ה', אות פו.
73. אבן העזר, סימן כ"ב, סעיפים א', ב'.
74. שם, סעיף ה', ברמ"א, חכמת אדם, כלל קכ"ו, סעיף ה'.
75. שם.
76. חכמת אדם שם.
77. אבן העזר שם, סעיף ט'.
78. שם, סעיף י"א.
79. ים של שלמה, קידושין סימן כ"ב, ב"ח, אבן העזר סימן כ"ג.
80. אבן העזר סימן כ"ב, סעיף א', חלקת מחוקק שם, ס"ק א'.
81. פתחי תשובה שם, ס"ק ב'.
82. אבן העזר שם, סעיף ט'.
83. ספר דבר הלכה על הלכות איסור יחוד, סימן ג', ס"ק ב'.
84. שם, סימן ג', ס"ק ג'.

85. אבן העזר, סימן כ"א, סעיף ז'.
86. בית שמואל שם, ס"ק י"ד, פתחי תשובה שם, ס"ק ה'.
87. בית שמואל שם, ס"ק ט'.
88. אבן העזר שם, סעיף ז'.
89. בית שמואל שם, ס"ק ט', אבן העזר, סימן כ"ב, סעיף י"א.
90. אורח חיים, סימן ע"ה, סעיף ה'.
91. חיי אדם, כלל ד', סעיף ב', משנה ברורה, סימן ע"ה, ס"ק ג'.
92. אבן העזר, סימן קט"ו, סעיף ד'.
93. שו"ת אגרות משה, יורה דעה, חלק ג', סימן ס"ח, ס"ק ד'.
94. ביאור הלכה, אורח חיים, סימן ע"ה, סעיף א', ד"ה „טפח מגולה".
95. חזון איש, אורח חיים, סימן ט"ז, ס"ק ח', ד"ה „כ' במ"ב".
96. שערים המצויינים בהלכה, סימן ה', ס"ק י', שם, בקונטרס אחרון.
97. אבן העזר, סימן כ"א, סעיף ז', חלקת מחוקק שם, ס"ק י"ב, בית שמואל, שם, ס"ק ט"ו.
98. אוצר הפוסקים, אבן העזר, סימן כ"א, ס"ק י"א.
99. אבן העזר, סימן כ"א, סעיף ז', חלקת מחוקק שם, ס"ק י"ב, בית שמואל, שם, ס"ק ט"ו.
100. ביאור הלכה, אורח חיים, סימן ע"ה, סעיף א', ד"ה „טפח מגולה".
101. חזון איש, אורח חיים, סימן ט"ז, ס"ק ח', ד"ה „כ' במ"ב".
102. אבן העזר, סימן כ"א, סעיף ז'.
103. משנה ברורה, סימן ע"ה, ס"ק י"ז.
104. שו"ת אגרות משה, אורח חיים, חלק א', סימן כ"ו.
105. שו"ת שרידי אש, חלק ב', סימן ח'.
106. אורח חיים, סימן ר"מ, סעיף ו', משנה ברורה שם, ס"ק כ"ב.

Chapter Six

Chinuch and the Education of Children

The term chinuch has a broad meaning in halachic terminology, as well as a more restrictive interpretation. In its broad sense chinuch refers to the responsibility of parents to train their children in the observance of all the various mitzvot which guide the life of an adult Jew. This duty of parents has been discussed in the earlier chapters of this work. There is also a narrower translation of the word chinuch. In this second sense chinuch refers to the obligation of parents to educate their child in different fields of intellectual knowledge. According to Halachah parents are required, in the first instance, to teach their children Torah learning in all its various forms. In addition, they are obligated to educate their children in other areas of knowledge as well. This chapter will discuss the specific responsibility of parents in regard to educating children in these areas of endeavor.

Teaching One's Son Torah

The father of a boy is obligated to teach his son Torah. This duty is more stringent than the general requirement a father has to train his child in the observance of all mitzvot as a fulfillment of chinuch. Despite its obvious importance, the obligation to educate a child in observing mitzvot is only of rabbinic origin.[1] By contrast, the duty of a father to teach his son Torah is an actual Torah law rather than a rabbinic enactment.[2] This duty is derived from the verse in Deuteronomy, incorporated in the Shema, which commands that "you shall teach [the words of Torah] to your sons."[3] The Talmud states that women are exempt from this mitzvah.[4] This statement is accepted as binding Halachah by the poskim.[5] A clarification is, however, necessary here. It is only the actual process of teaching a son Torah from which mothers are exempt. They are expected to enable their sons to learn Torah by bringing them to school and helping them to study in other ways. They are rewarded for this by having a share in their son's Torah learning.[6]

The original intent of the Torah was to have each father personally teach his own son. This is clearly indicated by the verse in Deuteronomy. However, from the period of second Beit Ha-Mikdash onwards this task was entrusted to a professional class of teachers. This was due to the decree of Joshua ben Gamla, one of the High Priests of that era. Seeing that children who were fatherless were not being educated in Torah, this Jewish leader established a school system in every Jewish community for all children of elementary school age. The Talmud highly praises him for this action, which ensured quality Jewish education for all.[7] Under these conditions a father can fulfill his duty to teach his son Torah by paying his son's teacher to discharge this obligation. The teacher then becomes the father's *shaliach*, or agent, in fulfilling this mitzvah.[8]

Since this is so, a father is halachically required to pay for his son's Torah tuition.[9] Indeed, he can be compelled to contribute these funds against his will. If the father is absent and unreachable the beth din is entitled to take his money in his absence and spend it for this purpose.[10]

The obligation to teach Torah to one's son is not limited to a man's male descendants in the first generation. It also extends to a person's grandson and even to his great grandson.[11] The poskim state that when a boy's father is unable to pay for his son's education the grandfather is obligated to cover this expense. According to many opinions it makes no difference whether the grandson is the son of one's son or the son of one's daughter. Indeed, a great-grandfather is required to pay for his great-grandson's Torah tuition when the boy's father is unable to do so.[12] Other authorities hold that a man is only obligated to pay for the Torah education of his son's son, but not for that of his daughter's son or for a great-grandchild under any circumstances.[13]

Paying Tuition

The Talmud states that a father is only required to pay a teacher to teach his son the entire written Torah. Once he has accomplished this minimum he has fulfilled his legal obligation as a father. The son is then required on his own to continue his study of the Mishnah and the Oral Law.[14] This statement is codified as binding Halachah in the *Shulchan Aruch*.[15] The majority of poskim understand the written Torah in this case as meaning the entire text of the Tanach, in other words the books of Neviim and Ketuvim (Prophets and Writings), in addition to the Chumash, or Pentateuch.[16] Despite this, the accepted traditional practice has not conformed to this pattern for centuries. Once a boy completes the study of Chumash he goes on immediately to the Mishnah, entirely neglecting the systematic study of the rest of Tanach. By following this method of education the father seemingly did not fulfill his obligation to have his son taught the entire text of the Tanach. Siftei Kohen justifies this practice. He quotes the Rishonim who state that by the study of Talmud a person fulfills the requirement of learning Tanach. This is because the Talmud is filled with quotations from the verses of Tanach. Since this is true, when a father has his son taught Talmud he fulfills his obligation to have him instructed in Tanach.[17] This opinion is accepted by the later authorities.[18]

The poskim write that the Halachah which states that a father is not required to pay for his son's instruction in the Oral Law only applies to a man of limited means. However, a father who can afford to pay for such education is required to have his son taught both Mishnah and Talmud.[19] Rabbi Shneur Zalman of Liadi goes even further. He argues that nowadays all fathers, irrespective of their financial means, are obligated to pay tuition for their sons to study at least a good portion of the Talmud so that the boy can continue learning on his own.[20] This opinion is disputed by other authorities.[21]

Two further points should be noted. According to the accepted contemporary method of Torah education, a boy is not taught the entire Tanach as required by the *Shulchan Aruch*. He is, rather, directed to Talmud study after several years of education in Chumash. This practice is defensible using the logic of Siftei Kohen, who argues that Talmud study in this instance takes the place of Tanach.[22] If this is the case, a father is indeed required to pay for Talmud instruction, since he is certainly obligated to pay for his son's education in Tanach.

In addition, Rabbi Moshe Feinstein points out that the contemporary civil laws of compulsory education, which require children to be sent to school up to a certain age, have the effect of obligating parents to pay for their children's tuition in yeshivot or day schools until they reach that age. This is because if these children are sent to non-Jewish public schools a definite danger exists of their developing into irreligious Jewish adults. The environment of such schools is clearly hostile to Jewish observance and religious practice. Parents have the obligation of ensuring that their children grow up to be pious, God-fearing Jews. This obligation makes it mandatory for them to send their children to yeshivot so that they can avoid the negative influence of non-Jewish schools. Parents are therefore required to pay for their children's yeshiva tuition until the point at which they become free of the obligations of the laws of compulsory education.[23]

Age and Curriculum

Parents often ask what the appropriate age is for beginning their son's Torah education. The Talmud states that informal education should begin very early in life. From the time that a boy starts to speak he should be taught the verse *Torah tzivah* (Deuteronomy 33:4) and the first sentence of the Shema.[24] The *Shulchan Aruch* codifies this as binding Halachah. It adds that the father should gradually add further verses which he teaches to his son.[25] Rema states that when the child is three years old the parents should begin to familiarize him with the letters and vowels of the Hebrew alphabet.[26] All of this is, however, is meant to be informal education rather than rigorous study.[27] Formal schooling, as such, begins, according to the *Shulchan Aruch*, at age five or six. Five years is the appropriate age for a more mature child; a less advanced boy should wait until six before beginning school.[28]

The initial subject to be taught is, of course, the study of Chumash (the Pentateuch). Even though the Chumash begins with the account of the creation of the universe in Genesis, the poskim recommend that this should not be the first topic taught to children. They suggest that Chumash study begin with the laws of the sacrifices contained in Leviticus. This is based on the Midrash which states that the pure minds of children should first be introduced to the laws of purity dealt with in this section of the Torah.[29] It is sometimes suggested that rather than have children taught the actual text of the Torah a summary should be used. This, supposedly, would remove extraneous material and make it easier for children to master the topic. This approach has been rejected by later poskim as constituting unacceptable tampering with the words of the Torah. Children must be taught the verses of the Chumash exactly as they are written.[30]

The Mishnah stresses that the correct curriculum in Torah education is five years of study of Chumash and Tanach followed by five years of instruction in Mishnah. Only then should the study of Talmud be begun.[31] Again, Jewish educational practice has not conformed to this plan for many centuries. Instead it has been traditional for a boy to receive a few years of instruction in Chumash and then proceed immediately to the study of Talmud. Siftei Kohen points out that this practice can be defended, quoting the many Rishonim who state that by the study of Talmud a person fulfills his obligation to learn the entire Tanach, because the Talmud is filled with quotations from Tanach.[32] Rabbi Shneur Zalman of Liadi defends the contemporary system on other grounds. He states that the opinion of the Mishnah was only relevant in earlier generations when so much of Torah, even including the vowel signs of the Chumash and Tanach, was only learned by oral transmission. At that time many years had to be devoted to memorizing both the correct punctuation of the Tanach and the actual words of the Mishnah. Today, of course, when all of the Torah exists in written form, this is no longer necessary.[33] The same answer is given by later poskim.[34]

The *Shulchan Aruch* states that children should attend school for the entire day and a small part of the night. Through doing this they will become accustomed to the requirement of studying Torah both during the day and during the night.[35] They only days given to children as school vacation should be Yomim Tovim, festivals, and the latter part of Friday and Erev Yom Tov to prepare for the coming Sabbath and festival.[36] On Shabbat children should not be taught new material, but the day should be used to review with them what they have already learned.[37]

It is common in contemporary communities for some yeshivot and day schools to have no classes on Sundays and legal holidays. This is often done due to parental pressure. Parents desire that their children be given these days as a school vacation so that they can engage in family activities which they are unable to undertake at other times. It is difficult to justify this practice on halachic grounds in view of the sources previously quoted. Rabbi Moshe Feinstein argues strongly that yeshivot should teach Torah subjects on such days. He concludes that it is possible to give students part of these days off by not scheduling secular classes on them. In this way the demand for family recreation time can be met.[38] He notes in a different connection that days which are non-Jewish religious holidays, such as the last week of December, should never be designated as vacation time for religious schools. By doing this, the school administration and the parents are indirectly participating in the celebration of non-Jewish religious festivals.[39]

Torah Education for Girls

Until this point we have discussed the responsibility of parents to have their sons taught Torah. The question of educating girls in Torah is an entirely different issue. The Talmud tells us that a father is only obligated to teach his son Torah, but not to teach his daughter.[40] It further notes that a woman, unlike a man, has no obligation to study Torah, even on her own, as an adult.[41] In another passage the Talmud states that it is wrong for a father to teach Torah to his daughter.[42]

This position is accepted by the later poskim. The *Shulchan Aruch* states that one should not instruct his daughter in Torah. However, it quotes Rambam, who differentiates between the Written Torah, meaning the books of the Tanach, and the Oral Torah—the Mishnah and Talmud. The Written Torah should not be taught to a girl in the first instance, but if a father does instruct his daughter in that subject, he commits no crime thereby in an *ex post facto* sense. However, teaching a daughter the Oral Law is regarded as improper even once it has already been done.[43] Rema adds that, despite this, a woman is obligated to study the practical halachic laws which apply to her so that she will be able to lead a religiously observant life.[44] Later poskim note that since this is so, it is obvious that parents have an obligation to have their daughter instructed in these laws.[45] It should be noted that these laws include all the mitzvot women are obligated to observe, meaning the majority of the laws of the Torah.[46]

These halachic guidelines would seem to allow the instruction of girls in practical halachic laws which apply to them, but not in the study of any other branch of Torah knowledge. The contemporary practice of almost all girls' schools is, however, to teach other Torah subjects to their students as well as practical Halachah. This procedure can be justified on diverse grounds.

Turei Zahav observes that while the *Shulchan Aruch* states that in the first instance even the Written Torah should not be taught to women, the prevailing practice is to instruct them in this subject. He explains that the study of the text of the books of Tanach on a simple level is permitted for girls, even according to the opinion of the *Shulchan Aruch*. What is forbidden is delving into the subject in a deep scholarly fashion.[47]

Chinuch and the Education of Children 101

In contemporary times the majority of poskim have gone even further than the argument of *Turei Zahav*. They state that nowadays girls should be instructed in the Written Torah and the ethical teachings of the Mishnah and Talmud in exactly the same way that boys are taught. A leading exponent of this point of view is the Chofetz Chaim. He argues that the proscription on teaching these subjects to girls was made for a society where girls were kept in the protective environment of their parental home. Due to this they were not subject to outside secular influences and to the demands of secular education. Under contemporary conditions, when all these challenges commonly present themselves to Jewish girls, parents are not only permitted but actually required to have their daughters instructed in these subjects. If they do not do so, there is little chance that their daughters will grow up to be observant Jews.[48]

The one subject which the Chofetz Chaim does not allow girls to be instructed in is the legal, or halachic, portions of the Mishnah and Talmud. This part of the Oral Law remains, in his view, forbidden, in accordance with the decision of the *Shulchan Aruch*. Rabbi Moshe Feinstein, in a written response, agrees with this point of view. He states that girls' schools should not teach the text of the Mishnah to their students, since that subject is part of the Oral Law mentioned in the Talmud as forbidden for instruction to women. He allows the teaching of ethical or moralistic portions of the Mishnah to girls. However, these parts of the Mishnah, such as Pirkei Avot, are not legal in nature, and therefore girls' schools may use them for instruction.[49] Many girls' yeshivot and schools follow this point of view.

There are poskim who argue that even the legalistic portions of the Talmud may be taught to girls. Rabbi Chaim David Azulai, known as Chidah, points out that there have been many instances throughout Jewish history of women who were very knowledgeable in just this branch of Torah study. Obviously it was permitted for them to be taught this subject.[50] He argues that the prohibition on instructing girls in the Oral Law applies to the majority of women, who show no interest or ability to master this topic. However, when women do display a desire to learn this part of Torah and have the requisite mind for doing so, there is no reason why they should not be instructed according to their wishes.[51] Rabbi Chaim David Halevy follows this line of reasoning and broadens it. He states that under contemporary conditions, when girls attend high school and study secular subjects on a level which requires mental acuity and intellectual discipline, we may assume that they have the required abilities to also be taught Talmud in the same way that boys are. Since this is so, he permits girls' schools to teach all Torah subjects to their pupils just as boys' schools do.[52] There are girls' yeshivot and schools which follow this approach.

It should be noted that according to all opinions, parents are not required to teach their daughters Torah. The preceding discussion only focused on whether parents may do so, if they wish. Despite this, in today's world, according to many opinions, parents are obligated to pay tuition for their daughters' day school or yeshiva education, just as they must do for their sons. Rabbi Moshe Feinstein points out that this is true because of the contemporary laws of compulsory education, which require all children to be sent to school until they reach a certain age. It is obvious that if girls are sent to non-Jewish schools a definite danger exists of their developing into irreligious adults. Due to the environment of such schools it is extremely difficult to bring up children sent there as observant Jews. Parents have an undisputed obligation to raise their daughters to be pious, religous Jews. The only way they can be certain of attaining such a goal is by sending their girls to yeshivot or day schools. It is therefore obligatory for them to give their daughters such an education and to pay for it.[53]

Coeducation

It has traditionally been accepted within the Jewish community that children should be segregated by sex from the beginning of their formal education. Separate classes for boys and girls were almost universally the rule. In contemporary times certain groups have expressed a desire for coeducational Jewish schools. Many schools have been founded along these lines. Some of these institutions are elementary schools, others are high schools. Many other yeshivot and day schools continue to be separated by sex. Parents, obligated by the demands of chinuch to send their children to Torah schools, are commonly faced with the decision as to which type of school they should choose for them.

Many contemporary poskim argue strongly that the Halachah does not allow for coeducation in Torah schools. Rabbi Moshe Feinstein states that it is the obligation of chinuch itself, which makes it imperative that boys and girls be placed in separate classes, even in elementary school. This is because the *Shulchan Aruch* rules that adult men and women should not be overly familiar with one another. It is the duty of parents to train their children to observe this restriction, just as they must teach their sons and daughters to keep all other Torah laws. The way children are trained to appreciate this requirement is by sending them to separate-sex schools, or at least to classes segregated by sex.[54] Rabbi Ovadiah Yosef agrees with this analysis. He writes that mixed classes are unacceptable for the same basic reasons.[55]

Nonetheless, Rabbi Feinstein argues that in cases where it is impossible to establish separate day schools for each sex it is permissible for boys and girls to be taught in the same class. This is true in small communities that cannot support two schools. He states that this arrangement is acceptable for small children who are not yet old enough to be affected by physical temptation. Since it is unclear whether the duty of chincuh obligates parents to separate such young children from one another, they may rely on the lenient approach and send their children to mixed schools in this case.[56]

The age at which children cease to be young enough for mixed classes to be acceptable is somewhat unclear. Rabbi Feinstein writes that separate-sex classes are mandatory by the seventh grade, for when children have reached this age, physical temptation is normally a problem for them.[57] Rabbi Yosef accepts the same line of reasoning, but only allows mixed classes in hardship cases through the third grade. Past this point he finds no permissibility for coeducational classes under any circumstances.[58]

It is clear that these poskim not only forbid coeducational classes but also proscribe mixed recreational activities between boys and girls. Rabbi Feinstein points out that the latter type of activities are even more clearly forbidden than the former. This is because supervision by a teacher is always present in a class setting, but may well be absent on a recreational occasion. The challenge of temptation is therefore greater during such an activity.[59] Due to this reasoning he states that girls' schools and boys' schools should be built in different locations with an appreciable distance between them, so as to make certain that recreational activities between the sexes will not occur. Only if it is financially impossible to obtain two buildings may one structure be used for both schools. In such a case, separate entrances should be designated, if possible, for boys and girls. Care must also be taken that recess or play activities are not scheduled for the same time for both sexes. Similarly, the two sexes should eat lunch at different times or in different locations.[60]

Rabbi Yechiel Yaakov Weinberg disagrees strongly with this entire restrictive approach. He bases his argument for leniency on the educational principles and practices of German Orthodox Jewry in the past century and a half. Guided by its rabbinical leaders this community had a positive attitude towards coeducational activities, whether in a formal school setting or outside of such a setting. Rabbi Weinberg states that there is no halachic objection to mixing between the sexes as long as it does not lead to immoral thoughts or behavior. Only in a synagogue is a physical separation necessary under all circumstances. He further argues that in Westernized societies coeducational activities must be encouraged, since only through them can the more acculturated portion of Jewish youth be saved for Torah and Judaism. He supports this argument by citing the exemplary results German Orthodox institutions had in developing their student into religiously observant and pious adults. According to this approach, there is no restriction against coeducational classes or mixed recreational activities.[61]

A question related to the permissibility of coeducational classes is the permissibility of women teachers for male students. The Talmud states that a woman should not teach in a boys' elementary school because she comes into close contact with the fathers of her students. Such a relationship is inappropriate for members of the opposite sex.[62]

It is extremely common in the contemporary world for boys' yeshivot to employ female teachers in various educational capacities. It would seem that such a practice contradicts this Talmudic principle. Rabbi Feinstein argues that the contemporary prevailing pattern is defensible. He states that the Talmud only forbids having female teachers for boys when instruction is given in the teacher's home. However, when teaching is done elsewhere, especially in a public place such as a school, no prohibition exists. Rabbi Feinstein concludes that when the student are no longer young children but older boys, every effort should be made to find male teachers for them. In this case it is doubtful whether a female teacher may be employed.[63]

The Talmud similarly states that an unmarried man should not be hired as a teacher of girls. If he is married, however, this is permitted.[64] Some yeshivot do not abide by this ruling and do employ single men as teachers of girls. This policy can be defended according to the view of some poskim who note that in contemporary times the practice is to allow such actions. Again, these authorities argue that when instruction takes place in a public place, such as a school, the Talmudic prohibition does not apply. Such teaching is only forbidden in a private home or other inaccessible place.[65]

Teaching Secular Studies

The Halachah only requires a father to teach his son Torah. It says nothing about any obligation to instruct a child in other branches of learning. Despite this, parents generally wish to have their children taught secular subjects, to a greater or lesser degree, in addition to Torah knowledge. This is especially true in the modern world, where compulsory education laws make it obligatory on parents to have their children receive such instruction, at least up to a certain minimum age. Given these facts it is obviously necessary for parents to know what the attitude of Halachah is towards teaching children secular subjects.

It would seem that parents are not obliged to instruct children in these branches of knowledge, but they are also not prohibited from giving such instruction if they so wish. There is, however, one problem. Fathers are obligated to teach their sons Torah. The extent of Torah knowledge is so broad that even if one were to devote himself to its pursuit to the exclusion of everything else in life, he still would not easily be able to master all of it. Since this is so, it appears that fathers are not permitted to have their sons taught secular subjects. The time devoted to such studies can be construed as being stolen from that which should be used for Torah study. Of course, this argument does not apply to daughters. Since there is no overiding halachic imperative to teach girls Torah, there is obviously no problem in having them instructed in the various branches of secular knowledge.

The *Shulchan Aruch* states that an adult male Jew is permitted to study the secular branches of knowledge. It makes the demand, however, that such studies be clearly secondary in time and importance to the individual's study of Torah. When secular studies are done in such a manner, they are not regarded as contradicting the duty of studying Torah which is incumbent on all Jews.[66] It seems clearly evident that the same principle can be applied to the education of boys. They too can be taught the secular disciplines, as long as these studies remain secondary to the primary pursuit of Torah knowledge on their part.

Rabbi Moshe Feinstein provides an additional reason for allowing yeshivot and day schools of the present age to teach secular subjects to their students. He points out that since contemporary parents demand such studies, and since the laws of compulsory education make them mandatory, children will certainly receive this type of instruction in some manner. If the yeshivot do not provide it, the children will be sent to non religious institutions for the study of these subjects. In such schools a good probability exists that the students will be influenced away from observant Judaism. It is therefore imperative that the religious schools offer such instruction within the confines of their walls. As long as these subjects are kept in a secondary position, no violation of Halachah occurs.[67]

This concern for keeping secular subjects in a secondary position for students must be taken seriously. It is common practice in most yeshivot and day schools to devote the morning hours to Torah studies and to reserve the second part of the day for other subjects. In some cases, however, schools mix the hours of these subjects so that certain classes wind up studying Torah in the afternoon and secular subjects in the morning. Rabbi Feinstein argues that such practices should be actively discouraged. When Torah is studied at the beginning of the school day the students are impressed with the idea that this should be their primary field of interest. When the reverse occurs, children can be led to believe that it is the non-Torah subjects which are the most important component of their education. Since one is only permitted to pursue secular knowledge as a secondary part of one's education, the school day must be structured to agree with this halachic imperative.[68]

Teaching a Child a Livelihood

As mentioned earlier, Halachah does not obligate a parent to teach his child secular knowledge. Torah is the only intellectual field in which a father is required to train his son. The Talmud does, however, state that a father is obligated to teach his son a livelihood so that he will be able to support himself as an adult. This requirement is mentioned together with the father's obligation to instruct his son in Torah.⁶⁹ The early poskim cite this requirement as binding on a father.⁷⁰ The *Shulchan Aruch*, obviously with this in mind, states that a father is even permitted to enter an arrangement on Shabbat for a man to teach his son a livelihood, since by doing so the father is fulfilling a mitzvah which is incumbent on him.⁷¹ *Magen Avraham*, in another connection, quotes the actual words of the Talmud as binding Halachah. He states that a father is obligated by Jewish law to teach his son a livelihood.⁷² Later poskim agree with this position.⁷³

It should be mentioned that despite all this, some poskim argue that the duty to teach one's son a livelihood is not a universal obligation which applies to all children equally. According to this opinion, this obligation is mandatory on a father for his average children. However, if a father has a son with outstanding intellectual abilities in Torah, he is not obligated to teach that child a livelihood. In such a case, the father should rather devote his son's education exclusively to Torah in the hope that his child will become a future Torah leader in the Jewish community.⁷⁴

The Talmud, when it states that a father must teach his son a livelihood, adds that some opinions require a father to teach his son how to swim. This is considered necessary because it can on occasion be life saving.⁷⁵ It is unclear whether or not this opinion is accepted as binding law by the later poskim. Since this is so, one contemporary authority considers it praiseworthy to instruct a child in this skill even though it cannot be unquestionably proven that an absolute requirement exists for a parent to do so.⁷⁶

Notes

1. חגיגה דף ו', עמוד א', שולחן ערוך הגרש"ז, הלכות תלמוד תורה, פרק א', סעיף א'.
2. יורה דעה, הלכות מלמדים, סימן רמ"ה, סעיף א'.
3. טור, יורה דעה, שם.
4. קידושין, דף כ"ט, עמוד ב'.
5. טור יורה דעה, סימן רמ"ה, בית יוסף שם, ד"ה „ואשה אינה חייבת".
6. סוטה, דף כ"א, עמוד א', דרכי משה, יורה דעה, סימן רמ"ה, ס"ק ב', שולחן ערוך הגרש"ז, הלכות תלמוד תורה, פרק א', סעיף י"ד.

Chinuch and the Education of Children

7. בבא בתרא, דף כ"א, עמוד א'.
8. ערוך השולחן, יורה דעה, סימן רמ"ה, סעיפים ה', ו', ז'.
9. יורה דעה שם, סעיף ד'.
10. שם, ש"ך שם, ס"ק ב.
11. שם, סעיף ג', ש"ך שם, ס"ק א'.
12. ש"ך שם, חכמת אדם, כלל ק"ד, סעיף י"ד, ערוך השולחן, יורה דעה, סימן רמ"ה, סעיף ט'.
13. שולחן ערוך הגרש"ז, הלכות תלמוד תורה, פרק א', סעיף ח'.
14. קידושין דף ל', עמוד א'.
15. יורה דעה, סימן רמ"ה, סעיף ו'.
16. ש"ך שם, ס"ק ה', ביאור הגר"א שם, ס"ק י"ד.
17. ש"ך שם, ס"ק ה'.
18. ביאור הגר"א, יורה דעה, סימן רמ"ו, ס"ק ט"ז, ערוך השולחן, יורה דעה, סימן רמ"ה, סעיף י"ג.
19. יורה דעה, סימן רמ"ו, סעיף ו'.
20. שולחן ערוך הגרש"ז, הלכות תלמוד תורה, פרק א', סעיף ו'.
21. ערוך השולחן, יורה דעה, סימן רמ"ה, סעיפים ג', ד'.
22. ש"ך שם, ס"ק ה'.
23. שו"ת אגרות משה, יורה דעה, חלק ב', סימן קי"ג.
24. סוכה דף מ"ב, עמוד א'.
25. יורה דעה, סימן רמ"ה, סעיף ה'.
26. יורה דעה, שם, סעיף ח', ברמ"א.
27. ערוך השולחן שם, סעיף ב'.
28. יורה דעה שם, סעיף ח'.
29. ש"ך שם, ס"ק ח'.
30. שו"ת צפנת פענח, סימן ס'.
31. מסכת אבות, פרק ה', משנה כ"א.
32. ש"ך יורה דעה, סימן רמ"ה, ס"ק ה'.
33. שולחן ערוך הגרש"ז, הלכות תלמוד תורה, פרק א', סעיפים א', ו'.
34. ערוך השולחן, יורה דעה, סימן רמ"ה, סעיף י"ג.
35. יורה דעה שם, סעיף י"א.
36. שם, סעיף י"ב, ש"ך שם, ס"ק ט', ט"ז שם, ס"ק ד'.
37. שם, סעיף י"ד.
38. שו"ת אגרות משה, יורה דעה, חלק ג', סימן פ"ד.
39. שם, סימן פ"ה.
40. קידושין דף ל', עמוד א'.
41. שם, דף כ"ט, עמוד ב'.
42. סוטה, דף כ"א, עמוד א'.
43. יורה דעה, סימן רמ"ו, סעיף ה'.
44. שם, ברמ"א.
45. ערוך השולחן, יורה דעה, סימן רמ"ו, סעיף י"ט.

46. שולחן ערוך הגרש"ז, הלכות תלמוד תורה, פרק א', סעיף י"ד.
47. ט"ז, יורה דעה, סימן רמ"ו, ס"ק ג'.
48. חפץ חיים, ליקוטי הלכות, סוטה, דף כ', עמוד א'.
49. שו"ת אגרות משה, יורה דעה, חלק ג', סימן פ"ז, חלק ב'.
50. שם הגדולים, מערכת גדולים, רבנית.
51. טוב עין, סימן ד'.
52. שו"ת עשה לך רב, חלק ב', סימן נ"ב.
53. שו"ת אגרות משה, יורה דעה, חלק ב', סימן קי"ג.
54. שו"ת אגרות משה, יורה דעה, חלק א', סימן קל"ז.
55. שו"ת יחוה דעת, חלק ד', סימן מ"ו.
56. שו"ת אגרות משה, יורה דעה, חלק א', סימן קל"ז.
57. שו"ת אגרות משה, יורה דעה, חלק ג', סימן ע"ח.
58. שו"ת יחוה דעת, חלק ד', סימן מ"ו.
59. שו"ת אגרות משה, יורה דעה, חלק ג', סימן ע"ט.
60. שם.
61. שו"ת שרידי אש, אורח חיים, סימן ח'.
62. קידושין דף פ"ב, עמוד א'.
63. שו"ת אגרות משה, יורה דעה, חלק ג', סימן ע"ג.
64. קידושין, דף פ"ב, עמוד א'.
65. ספר דבר הלכה על הלכות יחוד, סימן י"ב, ס"ק ה', ו', ז'.
66. יורה דעה, סימן רמ"ו, סעיף ד', ברמ"א.
67. שו"ת אגרות משה, יורה דעה, חלק ב', סימן פ"א.
68. שו"ת אגרות משה, יורה דעה, חלק ג', סימן פ"ג.
69. קידושין דף כ"ט, עמוד א'.
70. רי"ף שם, רא"ש שם, סימן מ"ג.
71. אורח חיים, סימן ש"ו, סעיף ו'.
72. מגן אברהם, סימן קנ"ו, ס"ק ב'.
73. ערוך השולחן, שם, סעיף א'.
74. שו"ת עשה לך רב, חלק ו', סימן פ"ז.
75. קידושין, דף ל', עמוד ב'.
76. מקור חיים השלם לרב חיים דוד הלוי, פרק ר"נ, סעיף ז', אות 15.

Chapter Seven

The Care of Children and Halachah

Jewish parents have three basic duties to their children, according to Halachah. In the first place, they are obligated to train their offspring in the observance of all the various mitzvot as a fulfillment of the duty of chinuch. This training is meant to ensure that when the child becomes a Jewish adult he or she will faithfully follow these commandments. Secondly, parents must see to it that their children are educated in Torah knowledge. This obligation was described fully in the preceding chapter. There is, in addition, a third responsibility which is incumbent on Jewish parents. Halachah requires that parents take proper care of their sons and daughters and make sure that their needs are met. There are times when this responsibility can come into conflict with other halachic guidelines or with prevailing social mores. Parents must be sure that in such cases they faithfully follow the decision of Halachah about the actions which they take.

The Obligation to Provide for Children

A Jewish father is halachically required to provide adequate food for his children. This obligation begins at birth and continues until the child reaches the age of six. If the father is unwilling to feed his child, the Jewish court is empowered to forcibly take his assets away and use them for this purpose. After the child reaches the age of six, the father is still required to provide for the child's food. However, in this case, if he fails to do so the court no longer has the power to take his possessions away from him and use them for this purpose. The religious authorities are, rather, required to publicly shame him and make him the object of communal scorn until he repents and agrees to meet his responsibility towards his children. If the father in question is wealthy, then the Jewish court is empowered to focibly use his assets to feed his children, even when they are above the age of six.[1] The same rules hold true in regard to providing clothing and shelter for one's children.[2]

The *Shulchan Aruch* states that once a man's children reach the age of Jewish adulthood the father no longer has a halachic obligation to support them. The age of adulthood is, of course, twelve for girls and thirteen for boys.[3] This should, however, not be understood as freeing parents under contemporary conditions from supporting their adolescent children. The later poskim point out that the *Shulchan Aruch* is speaking of its time, when the average child past the age of Jewish adulthood was able to provide for himself or herself. If, however, a child is unable to do this, then the father is required to meet those needs as a result of the obligation of charity.[4] Rabbi Moshe Feinstein argues that in today's world a father is halachically required to provide for his children until they reach the age when it is customary for them to go to work on their own. He traces this requirement to the obligations assumed by a husband to his wife at the time of their marriage.[5]

Charity and Children

The requirement to support one's children has further halachic ramifications. A Jew is required to give one-tenth of his yearly income to charitable causes. This tithe is known as *ma'aser ani*.[6] These causes can include any mitzvah activity, ranging from giving food and clothing to the poor to supporting the study of Torah.[7] Giving funds to one's children or parents, if they are genuinely in need, is considered to be a bona fide fulfillment of this obligation. Indeed, a person is supposed to put relatives ahead of strangers in the charity he gives.[8] The question which now exists is whether a man is permitted to count the money spent on supporting his children as part of the tenth of his income he is required to give to charity every year. In many cases, the amount used for food, clothing, and shelter for one's children equals and even exceeds the required *ma'aser ani*. This would mean that, in such cases, a father would have no further halachic obligation to give a tithe of his income to charity.

The poskim state that a person may not spend his *ma'aser ani* on a mitzvah which he is personally obligated to perform independently of the requirement to give charity. Thus, for example, he may not pay his communal taxes from *ma'aser ani*, even though these funds are used for mitzvah purposes. This is because payment of taxes is an obligation separate and distinct from the requirement to give charity.[9] A father is halachically obligated to support his children under the age of six to the extent that the beth din is empowered take away his money for this purpose. Since this is so, it is clear that funds used for this purpose cannot be counted as part of *ma'aser ani*. Preexisting personal obligations cannot be payed with charity money. *Turei Zahav* argues that this is true even in regard to funds used for supporting children above the age of six. There too, a father may not deduct such payments from his *ma'aser ani*.[10] *Siftei Kohen* disagrees. He states that money spent on supporting children above the age of six is no different than funds given to one's poor adult children. The father cannot be forced by the beth din to give such support. Since this is true, when he does donate these amounts he is fulfilling the mitzvah of charity and may count them as part of his yearly tithe.[11]

Some of the later poskim have decided in agreement with *Turei Zahav*. They state that it is not permissible to count money spent on supporting one's children above the age of six as *ma'aser*.[12] *Chochmat Adam* writes that as long as one's children live at home and are supported by their parents, the money used for their needs cannot be counted as *ma'aser*.[13] Rabbi Feinstein argues that, until children reach the age at which it is customary for them to go to work, a father cannot spend his *ma'aser* on their support.[14] Other poskim disagree. Chidah notes that the popular custom is to count such expenses as part of *ma'aser ani*.[15] Rabbi Ovadiah Yosef claims that is is perfectly acceptable for a father to consider all the money spent on the support on his children above the age of six as *ma'aser*.[16]

A related issue concerns the permissibility of paying for a child's yeshiva tuition out of a parent's *ma'aser* money. Rabbi Feinstein argues that a person may not do this. He states that parents are halachically obligated to finance the yeshiva schooling of their children, whether male or female, until they are past the age of compulsory education. This ensures that the children do not fall victim to the irreligious influence of secular schools. Since this is so, parents may not count money spent in fulfillment of this halachic obligation as part of their tithe given to charity.[17] Rabbi Yosef disagrees. He writes that once a father has paid for the expenses of his son's elementary yeshiva education, he may certainly count the money he spends on his son's further Torah tuition as part of his *ma'aser ani*.[18]

Nursing

Providing adequate nutrition is one of the primary responsibilities which parents owe to their children. During the first months of life infants do not, of course, need solid food. They require a liquid diet. Until the present century this diet universally consisted of breast milk. Nowadays, the alternative use of baby formula is possible. Nevertheless, many mothers continue to nurture their babies with breast milk for the early months of their life.

Halachah regards breast milk as a kosher substance. There is no restriction, as such, on consuming human breast milk.[19] Nevertheless, an adult is rabbinically forbidden to drink this milk directly from a woman's breast. The milk must first be drawn out into a vessel and then consumed.[20] By Torah law, breast milk, unlike the milk of kosher mammals, may be cooked with meat. It is, however, rabbinically prohibited to do this, since it may appear that one is cooking forbidden milk and meat together.[21] There is a debate among the poskim about whether human milk is considered the same as animal milk in regard to other prohibitions, such as waiting after meat before drinking milk.[22]

An infant is not included in the rabbinic prohibition regarding drinking human milk from the breast. The *Shulchan Aruch* states that a healthy child is permitted to be breast fed up to the age of four and a sickly child until the age of five. When these ages are reached, nursing must be ended. Even before this time, there are instances when it is forbidden to nurse from the breast. Once a child is twenty-four months old and has been removed from breast feeding for a period of three days or longer, it is forbidden to return him to the mother's breast. This rule, however, does not apply to a child younger than twenty-four months. A baby of less than two years may always be returned to breast feeding, no matter how long he has been taken away from this form of nursing.[23] The *Shulchan Aruch* further observes that a child is permitted to be nursed by a non-Jewish woman just as he may be by a Jewish wet nurse. Nevertheless, it is recommended that non-Jewish women not be used for this purpose. This is because non-Jews eat non-kosher food, which will have an unwholesome effect on the child through their milk.[24]

Breast feeding can cause problems on Shabbat or festivals. There is no doubt that is is permissible to nurse a child in the normal way on these days. It is, however, forbidden by Torah law to express milk from the breast into a vessel on Yom Tov or Shabbat to feed the baby later.[25] If a baby is unable or unwilling to nurse directly from the breast on these days, the mother is permitted to spray milk from the nipple into the baby's mouth.[26] If this method is unsatisfactory, a non-Jew may be asked to express the milk needed.[27] When all else fails, the mother may herself remove milk from the breast by hand or with a pump. This is because the baby is considered to be endangered without his mother's milk to which he has become accustomed.[28]

If the mother is bothered by an excess of milk in the breasts on Shabbat or Yom Tov, she is permitted to extract the milk by hand as long as the milk is poured on the ground or goes to waste in another way.[29] Some poskim permit a breast pump to be used in this case, provided that the pump is emptied of the accumulated milk at frequent intervals.[30]

Diapers

Taking care of infants and small children involves using diapers and disposing of them. The presence of dirty diapers in a house can cause halachic problems. This is because it is forbidden to pray, make a blessing, or utter words of Torah in the presence of human excrement. These activities are holy and can only be done in a place where it is appropriate for the name of God to be mentioned.[31] Parents who have infants and small children in the house are obviously faced with the question of performing such actions in a place which contains these problematic substances.

The *Shulchan Aruch* states that the excrement of a very small child is not included in this prohibition. Prayer and Torah study may be conducted despite the proximity of such substances. As long as a child cannot eat a *kezayit* of grain within a stated period of time, he is included in this permissible category.[32] The period of time required for this test is subject to debate. It is either the number of minutes it takes an adult to eat three eggs or four eggs.[33] Later poskim state that, as a general rule, once a child is one year old, he may no longer be assumed to be in this permissible category. From that point on, his excrement must be treated like that of an adult. Prayer and Torah study cannot be conducted near such substances.[34]

It would seem from this discussion that dirty diapers and soiled clothing of infants below the age of one do not constitute a problem for prayer and Torah study by parents. This is true in a strict halachic sense. However, the poskim state that it is appropriate, although not mandatory, to avoid the excrement even of a newborn when one is engaged in holy activities, just as one avoids

The Care of Children and Halachah 117

the excrement of an adult. The purity of these actions is impaired even by such conditions.[35]

One should not think that in view of these halachic guidelines it is impossible for parents to carry on prayer and Torah study in a house containing dirty diapers and soiled clothing. When excrement is covered, so that it is not open to the air, there is no prohibition on peforming any sacred actions in its presence.[36] The one exception to this rule is a case where a person can smell the offensive odor. When this happens, one is not permitted to pray or study Torah. In such a case, there is an argument as to what is required. Some opinions say that once a person is so far from the excrement that he can no longer smell it, he is permitted to perform these actions. Others say that he must go an additional distance of four *amot*, or cubits, past this point. However, all agree that if these conditions are met all holy activities may be carried out.[37]

In accordance with these rules, it is clear that if dirty diapers or soiled clothing are placed in a closed container it is completely acceptable for prayers to be said and Torah to be learned, as long as no offensive smell can be detected in the place in which these actions are being carried out. This is certainly true when the container is placed in a different room. The same rule will apply to children who are wearing dirty diapers. Since the excrement is covered, all sacred activities may be performed in their presence, as long as no offensive smell is noticed. Once such an odor is detected these actions must be stopped. They can only be continued in a place removed from the offensive smell.

A diaper pail is considered to be similar to a bed pan. It has the halachic status of excrement. Sacred activities may not be carried on in its presence, even when it contains no dirty diapers.[38] This is true of a receptacle made of wood or porcelain. One constructed out of glass or metal or having a glazed surface is not forbidden as long as it is washed and thoroughly clean.[39] It is unclear what the status of plastic pails will be. Certainly, if the pail is closed off in a separate room no problem exists. The same question exists in regard to a child's potty. Rabbi Moshe Feinstein argues that cloth diapers, once they are machine washed, are no longer considered to be in the category of a bed pan. Since they are cleaned like new, they are considered to be ordinary cloth. As long as they remain clean, all holy activities may be performed in their presence.[40]

Diapers on Shabbat and Yom Tov

The use of diapers for small children presents special problems on Shabbat and Yom Tov. Two of the forbidden labors on these days are fastening and unfastening. It is obviously necessary, in order to properly care for a child, that diapers be fastened so that they hold onto the child. It is similarly essential that diapers be removed from the child when required. The question is how such actions can be justified within the parameters of these forbidden labors on Shabbat and festivals.

Rabbi Moshe Feinstein argues that attaching two garments together, or two parts of one garment to one another, by pins is not included in the forbidden labor of fastening. The type of fastening forbidden on Shabbat and Yom Tov is when two garments, or two parts of one garment attached together, become like one. However, when they remain distinct and identifiable from one another, as they do when pins are used, no violation of the Shabbat or festival occurs. He concludes that there is therefore no problem in fastening or opening diapers with pins.[41] Other poskim permit this to be done because the diapers are only being attached temporarily for a short space of time. They argue that fastening is only forbidden when it is done to last for a substantial amount of time.[42] Rabbi Shlomo Zalman Braun argues that it is similarly permissible to use disposable diapers fastened by paper stickers on Shabbat and festivals. This is because the diapers are only fastened for a short space of time and the method used to attach them is one requiring no special skill. Such fastening or unfastening is not forbidden on Shabbat or Yom Tov.[43]

Cloth diapers which are dirty, or children's clothing or bedding which is soiled, may not be soaked in water on Shabbat or Yom Tov. This is because when a person puts water on dirty garments he is considered to be washing them. This is a violation of Shabbat or the festivals.[44] After the excrement is removed from the diapers, therefore, they cannot be put into water to soak. Some poskim permit a few drops of disinfectant to be shaken onto the diapers in the diaper pail in this case.[45] When disposable diapers are used, no such problem exists.

Rubber or nylon baby pants or a rubber or totally synthetic crib mattress may be soaked on Shabbat or Yom Tov if soiled. This is because the *Shulchan Aruch* says that no prohibition of washing exists in regard to leather. Modern poskim state that rubber or synthetics may be compared to leather. Care must, however, be taken that no rubbing of the materials be done while they soak in the water. In addition, soaking should only be done when the intention is to use these items on Shabbat or Yom Tov.[46]

Children's Body Care on Shabbat and Yom Tov

One of the most important aspects of caring for a child is the attention given to keeping the child's body and skin clean. Many of the actions done to achieve this goal raise halachic problems on Shabbat and Yom Tov. Observant parents are required to be aware of what actions are prohibited on these days in order to satisfy Jewish law while caring for their children.

One of the most basic aspects of keeping a child clean is the proper cleansing of the body and skin after dirty diapers are removed. This cleaning is often done with a sponge or wet cloth. This method cannot be used on Shabbat or festivals. It is forbidden on these days to use a wet cloth or sponge for wiping. This is because one will necessarily squeeze some of the water out of the wet cloths while using them for this purpose, and squeezing constitutes a violation of Shabbat or Yom Tov.[47] Rabbi Moshe Feinstein states that no problem of squeezing exists in connection with wet paper towels or tissues.[48] Since this is so, parents should use wet paper tissues for cleaning a baby's diaper area on Shabbat and festivals. In this way, no prohibition is incurred. Several varieties of prepared wet paper towels are commercially available for this purpose.

It should be noted that water may not be heated on Shabbat. Warm water used for cleaning children on that day must be heated prior to Shabbat and kept hot during the course of the day. There are various popular ways of doing this. A kettle filled with water can be left on the range throughout Shabbat provided that the stove top is covered with a blech, or metal plate, under which the fire is left burning.[49] Alternatively, an electric water heater can be filled before Shabbat and left plugged in throughout the day. Hot water can then be taken from this appliance.[50] The hot water collected in such ways can then be mixed with cold tap water in order to obtain water with the desired temperature. The proper way for this to be done is for the hot water to be placed in a container first and then for the cold water to be added. The hot water should not be poured from the kettle or electric heater onto cold water which has already been poured into a mixing container. In such a case a violation of Shabbat occurs.[51] It is never permissible for hot water to be taken from the faucet on Shabbat. Doing this constitutes a violation of the Sabbath.[52] Since cooking is permitted on Yom Tov, none of these restrictions apply on festivals. On those days hot water may always be taken directly from the faucet.[53]

Bathing a child, of course, constitutes the most important method for keeping that child clean and healthy. It is quite common to give a child a bath every day. On Shabbat this cannot be done. It is rabbinically forbidden to wash a person's entire body on Shabbat with warm water, even if the water used was boiled prior to Shabbat.[54] There is, however, no prohibition on washing parts of the child's body, such as the face and hands, with water heated prior to Shabbat.[55] In a case of necessity it is permissible to wash the child's entire body with this kind of water on Shabbat.

Necessity here does not mean actual illness. If the child is very uncomfortable, it is considered sufficient grounds to allow this procedure to be done.[56]

On Yom Tov it is also normally not permissible to wash one's entire body. However, if parents are accustomed to bathing a child every day, they are permitted to bathe him on Yom Tov as well. This is not true if they occasionally skip the bath for two or three days. In such a case, the bath is not considered essential enough to be given on the festival.[57] When parents are allowed to bathe the child on Yom Tov, they are not permitted to boil water on that day expressly for this purpose. They must, rather, use water heated for other permissible uses on the festival for the child's bath.[58] This problem does not exist in regard to water taken from contemporary boilers which provide hot water for the entire house. In this case, hot water can be taken directly from the faucet for the child's bath when bathing is permitted.[59]

It must be noted that when washing a child on Shabbat or Yom Tov neither a sponge nor a washcloth may be used. Otherwise the prohibition of squeezing will be violated.[60] In addition, solid soap may not be used on these days.[61] Some poskim forbid washing with liquid soap as well.[62] However, contemporary practice is to follow the opinions which permit the use of liquid soap during these times.[63]

An important part of body hygiene for babies is the use of oil or ointment on the child's skin. It is forbidden on Shabbat or Yom Tov to rub ointment into skin. This is considered to be a Torah violation on these days.[64] It is similarly prohibited to use thick oil, which does not flow freely, for this purpose. Light oil, which does flow freely, may, however, be rubbed into a child's skin.[65] An adult is prohibited from using such oil on himself unless he is actually sick.[66] However, a child is always considered to be potentially sick if deprived of his legitimate needs. Therefore, light oil can be used on his skin even if the skin is not presently irritated.[67]

When rubbing oil into skin on Shabbat or Yom Tov it is forbidden to pour the oil onto absorbent cotton and then spread it over the skin. This is because some of the oil will be squeezed out of the cotton during this process. Such squeezing is a violation of Shabbat or Yom Tov.[68] It is, however, permissible to put the oil on the baby's skin by hand and then spread it gently over the body using a piece of cotton for this purpose.[69]

If the child's skin is so sore that ointment is absolutely required, the ointment should be placed on a piece of cotton prior to Shabbat or Yom Tov. The cotton ball with the ointment may then be touched to the sore area as long as no attempt is made to rub the salve into the skin.[70] It should be noted that tearing of cotton into usable pieces is not permitted on Shabbat or Yom Tov. Parents should prepare all the cotton balls which will be needed on Shabbat or festivals prior to the onset of these days. They then may use the previously torn cotton as needed.[71]

Food Preparation on Shabbat and Yom Tov

The preparation of food is obviously one of the most important ways in which parents care for their offspring. Different aspects of food preparation for children present halachic problems on Shabbat and Yom Tov. The observant parent is required to be familiar with these matters and to deal with them in a manner whereby he or she does not violate the sanctity of these days while seeing to the needs of his children.

The first food given to newborns is either breast milk or baby formula. The halachic complications which nursing with breast milk can cause have been discussed earlier in this chapter. The use of formula also presents various difficulties in regard to Shabbat and Yom Tov. Formula can be purchased in ready-to-eat state, liquid concentrate, or powder form. Cans containing any of these varieties may not be opened on Shabbat or Yom Tov. They must, rather, be opened prior to these days.[72] The contents may, of course, be emptied and placed in the refrigerator over Shabbat and Yom Tov. In a case where this was not done, a non-Jew may be asked to open the can. Even though normally this kind of request is not permitted, it can be allowed for the benefit of the infant who requires the formula. This is because such a child is considered to be in the category of the sick, for whom such requests may be made.[73]

Preparing the ready-to-eat formula presents no further halachic problems. Both the liquid concentrate and the powder varieties must be mixed with water before they are given to the child. It is normally forbidden to measure foods in a measuring cup on Shabbat or Yom Tov. This must, however, be done for the formula to be made in the right proportions. It is permissible to do the necessary measuring in these situations, since every infant is considered to be in the category of the sick. The *Shulchan Aruch* explicitly states that measurements may be taken in an exact form on Shabbat for the needs of people in this category.[74] Mixing the powdered variety of formula with water to make it edible for the baby presents no halachic difficulty on Shabbat. Since the powder dissolves into the water merely by shaking the container and actual mixing with a spoon is not necessary, no violation of the prohibition of kneading on Shabbat occurs.[75]

No matter which variety of formula is used, the prepared bottle is generally warmed before being offered to the baby. On Shabbat the bottle cannot be heated under the hot water faucet. This is because this faucet cannot be used on Shabbat.[76] Hot water must be taken either from a kettle kept on the stove covered by a metal plate from before Shabbat[77] or from an electric water heater plugged in before Shabbat.[78] The baby's bottle can then be placed into a container filled with this water to be warmed.[79] Some poskim do not require the hot water to be poured into the container first. They allow the water to be poured directly from the kettle or the heater over the baby's bottle.[80] The same methods must be used to warm a milk bottle being prepared for a child. None of these restrictions apply to Yom Tov. Since cooking is permitted on festivals, hot water may be obtained from the faucet in the regular manner on these days, and the bottle can be warmed in the normal way.[81]

The preparation of baby cereal on Shabbat can also be the cause of halachic problems. Some of these questions are identical to those involving the use of formula. In the first instance, cereal boxes must be opened prior to Shabbat, just as must be done with formula cans. Again, the cereal powder may be measured prior to adding water if necessary, just as one may do with powdered formula. There is, however, one additional issue which is involved in making baby cereal on Shabbat. When a liquid is added to a solid and mixed with it so that a paste results, a violation of Shabbat is committed. The prohibited labor of *lishah*, or kneading, is performed.[82] This would seem to raise great problems for the use of baby cereal on Shabbat.

Despite this, it is permissible to make such cereal on Shabbat when two conditions are met. Firstly, the milk or juice must be added to the cereal powder in a manner different from the one usually employed. A person who normally puts the cereal into the mixing bowl first and then adds the liquid must do the reverse on Shabbat. The same is true, in an opposite sense, if he customarily pours liquid into the mixing bowl first. In such a case, he must place the cereal powder into the bowl before the milk or juice.[83] A person who is uncertain as to what his normal mixing procedure is should put the cereal in first and then add liquid. In addition, a change must be made in the actual mixing process. If possible, one should combine the cereal in first and then add liquid.[84] In addition, a change must be made in the actual mixing process. If possible, one should combine the cereal and milk or juice by using a finger[85] or by shaking the vessel rather than by utilizing a spoon.[86] If a spoon must be used for the cereal to come out right, then one must stir the spoon in a manner different from the usual method employed. Criss-cross motions should be used, rather than the normal circular stirring done with a spoon.[87]

Even when these conditions are met, it is usually forbidden to produce such a mixture if the result is a thick paste rather than a thin liquid-like combination.[88] However, this is not true when a thick mixture must be made fresh and cannot be prepared prior to

The Care of Children and Halachah

Shabbat. In such a case, a person may prepare this type of paste on Shabbat, as long as he conforms to the previously mentioned restrictions.[89] There is, therefore, no problem in making baby cereal on Shabbat, no matter what its consistency may be. On Yom Tov there is no prohibition on kneading and none of these limitations apply.[90] Obviously, this entire discussion applies in exactly the same way to the making of instant baby food on Shabbat by adding water to the baby food powder or to any other food of this type.

The final problem involving the preparation of food for young children on Shabbat or Yom Tov concerns grinding or mashing. It is never permitted to grind or chop food on Shabbat using a grater or instrument made specifically to do this task.[91] Parents who grind meat or other foods for their infants with a food mill must, therefore, be careful to do this before Shabbat. It is also fobidden to dice fruits or vegetables on Shabbat or to cut them up very finely. There is, however, no prohibition on cutting them into small pieces.[92] Rema states that the dicing of fruits and vegetables is permissible when done immediately prior to their being consumed. Only if this is done a long while before they are eaten is it a violation of Shabbat.[93] Some poskim disagree and argue that dicing is forbidden on Shabbat under all circumstances.[94] *Magen Avraham*, and many authorities who follow him, defend this practice, as long as it is done right before eating.[95] In the case of a child who has difficulty eating food unless it is diced finely, parents can rely on the lenient opinion and cut up the food in this way immediately before it is consumed.[96] According to all opinions foods which are not agriculturally grown, such as meat and fish, may be chopped finely on Shabbat without any limitations.[97]

It is similarly forbidden to mash raw fruits or vegetables on Shabbat. Some poskim argue that, unlike dicing, mashing may not be done even immediately prior to eating.[98] According to them, it is only permissible to mash when the method used is different than normal. A parent desiring to mash a banana for a child must, according to this view, use the handle of a fork or a spoon rather than the prongs of the fork. This constitutes an acceptable change from the normal procedure.[99] Other poskim disagree. They permit raw fruits and vegetables to be mashed in the normal way, as long as the process is done immediately prior to eating.[100] There is no limitation on crumbling bread or cake into powder on Shabbat for a child's use, provided that a grater is not used. This is because these items are made from ingredients which have already been ground up and later combined together.[101]

On Yom Tov fruits and vegetables may be diced, since doing so prior to the festival would cause them to lose some of their flavor.[102] A food grinder may, however, only be used if a change is made in its normal mode of operation. For example, the food should not be ground so that it falls into its usual receptacle. It should, rather, be made to fall onto a piece of paper or the top of the table.[103] Fruits and vegetables may be mashed on Yom Tov in the ordinary way.[104]

Transporting a Child

One of the forbidden labors of Shabbat is carrying objects through the public domain, such as a street, as well as moving objects from a private domain, such as a house or enclosed yard, to the street. This poses a problem for the observant Jewish parent who wishes to carry or transport his child from his house to the street or in the street itself. When he carries the child he violates the prohibition of carrying on Shabbat. The Talmud states that one who carries a living person is not guilty of violating Shabbat. This is because a live person is said to carry himself, since he makes himself lighter by having his own muscles share the burden of being carried.[105] This, however, does not mean that parents may carry their children on Shabbat. Such an action is rabbinically forbidden everywhere except within the confines of a house or enclosed yard.[106] In the case of a child who is too young to walk on his own, things are even more restrictive. A Torah violation of Shabbat is committed when such a child is carried. This is because we do not say that the child helps to carry himself.[107] This means that no permissibility exists for carrying a child on Shabbat in the public domain under normal circumstances. When a child is taken out in a carriage or stroller the same prohibition of carrying is violated.[108] None of these restrictions apply on Yom Tov. Children of all ages may be carried on these days in any manner desired.[109] Of course, when there is an eruv, the carrying of children on Shabbat is completely permissible.

Once a child is old enough to walk on his own, parents may take him for a walk on Shabbat. They must, however, be careful to allow him to walk by himself and not lift him or drag him along. It is, however, permissible to hold the child's hand and guide him along the desired route.[110] If the child refuses to continue walking the parents may lift him up, but they should not walk further with him. If this method of persuasion fails, a non-Jew may be asked to carry the child home.[111] This is often impractical, however, since many young children will refuse to be carried by strangers. In such a case, the parents may carry the child home. This is permissible because the majority of poskim consider carrying in most contemporary streets to be only a rabbinic prohibition.[112] In addition, carrying a child who can walk on his own is also only rabbinically forbidden.[113] The general rule is that one may violate rabbinic prohibitons on Shabbat to provide for the acute needs of a child. The parent, in this case, should attempt to carry the child home in a way different than normal if possible.[114] If this cannot be done, the parent may carry the child home in any way that is feasible.[115] Even when it is permissible to do this, parents must be sure that the child is not holding an object in his hands or his pockets while being carried. Such objects must be removed from the child before he may be carried.[116] Because of the probability of such halachic problems occurring, parents should not take children walking on Shabbat until they have adequate reasons to assume that the child will be able to return home on his own.

If a child who knows how to walk is sick and must be taken to the doctor, he may be carried there if it is difficult for him to walk. This is certainly true in a case of even the most remote danger to life, since all Shabbat laws are cancelled in such instances.[117] It is, however, also true in the case of an illness which is clearly not life-threatening. This is because one may always violate Shabbat rabbinic prohibitions to provide for the acute needs of a child.[118] Carrying a child who is able to walk is only a rabbinic prohibition, as mentioned earlier.

The case of an infant who is unable to walk is more complicated. Carrying such a child in the street is a Torah violation of Shabbat, rather than only a rabbinic offense.[119] A parent should try to have a non-Jew carry such an infant to the doctor. When a non-Jew does this, only a rabbinic violation of Shabbat takes place. If this is impossible, it is permissible for the parent himself to carry the sick infant, according to the majority of poskim who consider carrying in most contemporary streets to be only rabbinically forbidden.[120] Of course, carrying in a minority of today's streets can be a Torah violation. It would be forbidden for a parent to carry such an infant through the streets. Again, it must be emphasized that if even the remotest danger to life exists for the infant he may be carried by the parent without any question. The same rules that apply to an infant too young to walk also apply to an older child who is too sick to physically be able to walk.[121]

As mentioned previously, a baby carriage may not be taken out of the private domain on Shabbat, unless there is an eruv. When there is an eruv, or on Yom Tov, a parent may wheel a carriage in the street. However, one restriction remains on the use of such a vehicle. The hood of the stroller or carriage may not be opened on Shabbat or Yom Tov. When one does this, he creates an *ohel*, or tent, which is a violation of Halachah on these days.[122] Despite this, if the hood was left open the width of a *tefach*, or handbreadth, prior to Shabbat or Yom Tov, it may be opened to its full length. This is permissible because the *ohel* exists already. All that the person is doing is adding to it, which is allowed on these days.[123] It is similarly permitted to close the hood, as long as one *tefach* of its width is left open.[124] The same rules will apply to hanging a mosquito net over a carriage. If the hood has been left open the width of a *tefach* prior to Shabbat or Yom Tov, a net may be placed over the carriage on these days.[125]

It is always permissible to fold or open a collapsible carriage or stroller on these days. Since the vehicle already exists in its complete form and is merely being opened or closed, no violation of Shabbat or Yom Tov is committed by these actions.[125] A carriage or stroller does not have to be restricted to paved roads on Shabbat or Yom Tov. It may be wheeled over earth or sand without any concern that it may make marks in the ground. This is true no matter how large the carriage might be. There are varied halachic reasons for this fact.[127]

Medical Care of Children

The halachic rules which govern the care of the sick on Shabbat and Yom Tov are more lenient in the case of children than they are for adults. In halachic terminology, there are three categories of sick people on these days. The first group of the sick consists of those whose illness constitutes a possible threat to their lives. Shabbat or Yom Tov must be violated in any manner necessary to care for them, whether they are adults or children. This is true even if the danger to life is remote.[128] The second category of ill people consists of those who do not suffer from a sickness which can cause a danger to life, but are so ill that they are confined to bed. People whose whole body is in pain are also included in this category. It is permissible to ask a non-Jew to do anything necessary for these individuals. It is similarly permitted to violate rabbinic prohibitions to care for them, as long as the action taken is performed in a way different than that usually followed.[129] People suffering from ailments less severe than those described previously cannot have Shabbat or Yom Tov violated for them in any manner.[130]

In the case of a child, even a minor pain or ailment is sufficient to warrant being classified in the second category of the sick. This means that it is always permissible to ask a non-Jew to do whatever is necessary for a child who is even slightly ill. It is similarly permitted to violate all rabbinic prohibitions for a child who is mildly sick.[131] If possible, such violations should be done in a manner different from the normal way of performing these actions. However, if this is very difficult or impossible, it is permissible to perform the required action normally.[132] This leniency for children is not restricted to infants. It applies until the child reaches the age of nine.[133]

It is forbidden for an adult who is only mildly ill on Shabbat or Yom Tov to take medication for his illness.[134] It is similarly prohibited for such a person to consume foods or drinks as medicine, if these items are not normally eaten for other than medicinal purposes. In such a case, it is clear that the person is using the foods or drinks as medication. People who are confined to bed or whose whole body is in pain are not considered to be mildly ill. They may take medication on Shabbat or Yom Tov.[135] Children are always considered to be within the latter category. They can, therefore, be given medicine in any form on these days even for a slight illness or indisposition.[136]

Some poskim argue that vitamins are included in the prohibition of taking medicines for a slight illness on Shabbat or Yom Tov.[137] Others disagree. They point out that vitamins are taken not to cure sickness but to prevent it. Thus there is no restriction on consuming such substances on these days.[138] It is certain, according to all opinions, that children may be given vitamins on Shabbat or Yom Tov. This is because they are always considered to be within the category of the seriously ill who may be given medication on these days under all circumstances.[139]

If a child has a splinter in his skin it is permissible for the parent to remove it by the use of a needle or other appropriate instrument on Shabbat or Yom Tov. An attempt should be made to do this without causing the child to bleed. If, however, it is impossible to achieve this, the splinter may be removed in any case.[140] Although measuring is a forbidden activity on Shabbat and Yom Tov, this prohibition does not apply to using a thermometer to check on illness. Modern poskim agree that a thermometer may be used for adults on these days and certainly for children as well.[141] Of course, this refers to a simple thermometer rather than one which works through electricity or a fever strip which changes color. Using the latter instruments presents more serious halachic problems.

Babysitters and Teachers

The use of babysitters to watch children while parents are absent presents two separate halachic problems. It is forbidden for a Jew to pay a fellow Jew for work which the second person has done for him on Shabbat or Yom Tov. This is true even when the job done by the fellow Jew was a permissible activity on Shabbat or Yom Tov.[142] It is similarly prohibited to arrange for such an acitivity before Shabbat, even if the payment for it will only be given after Shabbat.[143] This presents a serious problem for parents who want to hire a babysitter to watch their children on Shabbat or Yom Tov. It would seem that there is no permissible way to pay such a person for her work.

There are two solutions to this difficulty. The *Shulchan Aruch* states that the prohibition does not apply when a person is given a lump-sum payment for a period of time in which Shabbat or Yom Tov are included. Only if the payment is given exclusively for these days does a violation of Halachah occur.[144] Therefore, if a babysitter is paid at one and the same time for babysitting done both on Shabbat and on weekdays the prohibition is not violated. Such an arrangement must be made with the babysitter from the beginning.

This solution will not work, of course, if the babysitter is only hired for Shabbat or Yom Tov. In such a case the problem can be circumvented by hiring a non-Jew. There is no prohibition against paying a non-Jew for work done on behalf of a Jew on these days, as long as the work itself was not forbidden labor.[145] This is obviously true in the case of babysitting.

Hiring a non-Jewish babysitter, however, presents a second difficulty. The Mishnah states that a Jew should not be alone with a non-Jew due to fear that the non-Jew may be bloodthirsty and kill him.[146] The *Shulchan Aruch* codifies this as binding Halachah.[147] Similarly, a Jewish baby should not be left alone with a non-Jewish nurse for the same reason, unless this is done in a Jewish home with other people present.[148] This would seem to make it a violation of Halachah for a non-Jewish babysitter to be hired. Later poskim point out that this is untrue today. These rules have not applied for many past centuries and do not have to be followed in the present day. The non-Jews whom the Mishnah is referring to were savage pagan idolators who were suspected of the lowest moral behavior. In contemporary times, when there is a strict regimen of laws which enforce civilized behavior, there is no reason to observe these restrictions.[149] Modern authorities have fully accepted this line of reasoning. There is no restriction today on leaving babies with non-Jews.[150]

There is, however, one problem in hiring non-Jews as babysitters. The *Shulchan Aruch* states that a Jewish child should not be placed in the care of a non-Jewish teacher, out of fear that he may be influenced to leave Judaism.[151] It would seem that this fear applies to the case of a child sent alone to a non-Jewish teacher's home. It is not applicable to the case of a babysitter who does not teach the child anything. Similarly, when a Jewish school employs non-Jewish teachers, this problem is minimized. In these cases, the teacher is left with a large group of students. In addition, the administration is present in the building. No state of yichud, of allowing an individual student to be alone with the non-Jew and his influence, occurs.[152] This is indeed the practice of most contemporary yeshivot and day schools, which employ such teachers on their professional staff with no hesitation.

Blessing Children

There can be no doubt that blessings given by parents to their children form part of the care which fathers and mothers lavish on their offspring. There is no halachic obligation for parents to bless their children. Nevertheless, a well-established custom exists in many Jewish communities for this to be done on special occasions. The evenings of Shabbat and Yom Tov, prior to making Kiddush, are one such time.[153] It is also customary for parents to bless their children immediately before going to Kol Nidre on Yom Kippur. At that time they pray that their children will be granted a year of blessing and grow up to be pious, God-fearing Jews.[154] It is common or the verses of the priestly blessing to be recited by parents on these occasions. Even though a non-kohen is forbidden to join the kohanim in giving the priestly blessing to the Jewish people, this practice is acceptable. Since the parents are not uttering the blessing during communal prayer, it is as if they specifically have it in mind not to fulfill the duty of kohanim in blessing the Jewish people. When they do this they commit no violation of Halachah.[155]

Notes

1. אבן העזר, סימן ע"א, סעיפים א', ב'.
2. שם, סימן ע"ג, סעיף ו', חלקת מחוקק שם, ס"ק ה'.
3. שם, סימן ע"א, סעיף א'.
4. בית שמואל שם, ס"ק ג', בית הלל שם, סעיף א'.
5. שו"ת אגרות משה, יורה דעה, חלק א', סימן קמ"ג.
6. יורה דעה, סימן רמ"ט, סעיף א'.
7. ש"ך שם, ס"ק ג', פתחי תשובה שם, ס"ק ב'.
8. יורה דעה, סימן רנ"א, סעיף ג'.
9. ט"ז, יורה דעה, סימן רמ"ט, ס"ק א', ש"ך שם, ס"ק ג', באר הגולה שם, ס"ק ה'.
10. ט"ז שם, ס"ק א'.
11. ש"ך יורה דעה, סימן רנ"א, ס"ק ד'.
12. ברכי יוסף, יורה דעה, סימן רמ"ט, ס"ק י"ח, ערוך השולחן שם, סעיף ז'.
13. חכמת אדם, כלל קמ"ד, סעיף י"א.
14. שו"ת אגרות משה, יורה דעה, חלק א', סימן קמ"ג.
15. ברכי יוסף, יורה דעה, סימן רמ"ט, ס"ק י"ח.
16. שו"ת יחוה דעת, חלק ג', סימן ע"ו.
17. שו"ת אגרות משה, יורה דעה, חלק א', סימן קמ"ג.
18. שו"ת יחוה דעת, חלק ג', סימן ע"ו.

19. יורה דעה, סימן פ״א, סעיף ז׳, ש״ך שם, ס״ק י״ז.
20. יורה דעה שם, ט״ז שם, ס״ק ט׳.
21. יורה דעה, סימן פ״ז, סעיף ד׳.
22. כף החיים שם, ס״ק כ״ט.
23. יורה דעה, סימן פ״א, סעיף ז׳.
24. שם.
25. פרי מגדים, אורח חיים, סימן שכ״ח, אשל אברהם, ס״ק מ״א, ביאור הלכה שם, ד״ה „ותניק את בנה".
26. אורח חיים, סימן שכ״ח, סעיף ל״ה.
27. ביאור הלכה שם, ד״ה „ותניק את בנה".
28. שמירת שבת כהלכתה, פרק ל״ו, סעיף כ״א.
29. אורח חיים, סימן ש״ל, סעיף ח׳.
30. שמירת שבת כהלכתה, פרק ל״ו, סעיף כ׳.
31. משנה ברורה, סימן ע״ו, ס״ק ב׳.
32. אורח חיים, סימן פ״א, סעיף א׳.
33. משנה ברורה שם, ס״ק ג׳.
34. כף החיים שם, ס״ק ו׳.
35. חיי אדם כלל ג׳, סעיף ח׳, משנה ברורה, סימן פ״א, ס״ק ג׳.
36. אורח חיים, סימן ע״ו, סעיף א׳.
37. אורח חיים, סימן ע״ט, סעיף ב׳, משנה ברורה שם, ס״ק י״ז.
38. אורח חיים, סימן פ״ז, סעיף א׳.
39. שם, משנה ברורה שם, ס״ק ה׳.
40. שו״ת אגרות משה, אורח חיים, חלק ד׳, סימן ק״ו, ס״ק ב׳.
41. שו״ת אגרות משה, אורח חיים, חלק ב׳, סימן פ״ד.
42. שו״ת מנחת יצחק, חלק ב׳, סימן י״ט.
43. שערים המצויינים בהלכה, קונטרס אחרון, סימן פ׳, ס״ק מ״ה.
44. משנה ברורה, סימן ש״ב, ס״ק ל״ט, נ״ה.
45. שמירת שבת כהלכתה, פרק ט״ו, סעיף ד׳.
46. שם, פרק ט״ו, סעיף ה׳.
47. מגן אברהם, סימן ש״ב, ס״ק כ״ז, משנה ברורה שם, ס״ק נ״ט.
48. שו״ת אגרות משה, אורח חיים, חלק ב׳, סימן ע׳.
49. שו״ת אגרות משה, אורח חיים, חלק א׳, סימן צ״ג.
50. שמירת שבת כהלכתה, פרק א׳, סעיף מ׳.
51. אורח חיים, סימן שי״ח, סעיף י״ב, משנה ברורה שם, ס״ק פ״א, פ״ב.
52. שמירת שבת כהלכתה, פרק א׳, סעיף ל״ט.
53. שם, פרק ב׳, סעיף ז׳.
54. אורח חיים, סימן שכ״ו, סעיף א׳.
55. שם.
56. ביאור הלכה שם, ד״ה „במים".

57. אורח חיים, סימן תקי"א, סעיף ב' ברמ"א, מגן אברהם שם, ס"ק ה', משנה ברורה שם, ס"ק י"ב.
58. אורח חיים שם, משנה ברורה שם.
59. שמירת שבת כהלכתה, פרק י"ד, סעיף ט'.
60. מגן אברהם, סימן ש"ב, ס"ק כ"ז, משנה ברורה שם, ס"ק נ"ט.
61. אורח חיים, סימן שכ"ו, סעיף י' ברמ"א.
62. שו"ת אגרות משה, אורח חיים, חלק א', סימן קי"ג.
63. ערוך השולחן, אורח חיים, סימן שכ"ו, סעיף י"א, שמירת שבת כהלכתה, פרק י"ד, סעיף ט"ז.
64. אורח חיים, סימן שי"ד, סעיף י"א.
65. שם, משנה ברורה שם, ס"ק מ"ה.
66. אורח חיים, סימן שכ"ז, ברמ"א.
67. שמירת שבת כהלכתה, פרק ל"ז, סעיף ו'.
68. אורח חיים, סימן ש"כ, סעיף ט"ז, משנה ברורה שם, ס"ק מ"ד.
69. שמירת שבת כהלכתה, פרק י"ד, סעיף כ"ח.
70. שם, פרק ל"ג, סעיף י"ג.
71. שו"ת מנחת יצחק, חלק ד', סימן מ"ה.
72. אורח חיים, סימן שי"ד, סעיף א', שו"ת אגרות משה, אורח חיים, חלק א', סימן קכ"ב.
73. אורח חיים, סימן שכ"ח, סעיף י"ז, ברמ"א.
74. אורח חיים, סימן ש"ו, סעיף ז', משנה ברורה שם, ס"ק ל"ו.
75. חזון איש, הלכות שבת, סימן נ"ח, ס"ק ט'.
76. שמירת שבת כהלכתה, פרק א', סעיף ל"ט.
77. שו"ת אגרות משה, אורח חיים, חלק א', סימן צ"ג.
78. שמירת שבת כהלכתה, פרק א', סעיף מ'.
79. אורח חיים, סימן שי"ח, סעיף י"ג.
80. שמירת שבת כהלכתה, פרק א', סעיף נ'.
81. שם, פרק ג', סעיף ז'.
82. משנה ברורה, סימן שכ"א, ס"ק נ'.
83. אורח חיים, סימן שכ"א, סעיף י"ד, משנה ברורה שם, ס"ק נ"ז.
84. אליה רבה, סימן שכ"א, ס"ק כ', משנה ברורה שם, ס"ק נ"ז.
85. אורח חיים שם, סעיף ט"ז ברמ"א.
86. אליה רבה שם, ס"ק כ"ב, משנה ברורה שם, ס"ק ס"ג.
87. חזון איש, הלכות שבת, סימן נ"ח, ס"ק ו'.
88. מגן אברהם, סימן שכ"א, ס"ק כ"ד, משנה ברורה שם, ס"ק ס"ו.
89. משנה ברורה שם, ס"ק ס"ח, שער הציון שם, ס"ק פ"ד.
90. אורח חיים, סימן תק"ו.
91. אורח חיים, סימן שכ"א, סעיף י'.
92. שם, סעיף י"ב.
93. רמ"א שם.
94. חיי אדם, כלל י"ז, סעיף ב', משנה ברורה, סימן שכ"א, ס"ק מ"ה.

95. מגן אברהם, סימן שכ"א, ס"ק ט"ו, משנה ברורה שם, ס"ק מ"ה.
96. שמירת שבת כהלכתה, פרק ו', סעיף ו', תשובת הגר"מ פיינשטיין על הלכות שבת לרב איידער, חלק ד', סימן ב'.
97. אורח חיים, סימן שכ"א, סעיף ט', משנה ברורה שם, ס"ק ל"א.
98. שם, סעיף ז'.
99. חזון איש, הלכות שבת, סימן נ"ז, ד"ה „נמצינו", שמירת שבת כהלכתה, פרק ו', סעיף ח'.
100. תשובת הגר"מ פיינשטיין על הלכות שבת לרב איידער, חלק ד', סימן ב'.
101. אורח חיים, סימן שכ"א, סעיף י"ב, משנה ברורה שם, ס"ק מ"ה.
102. חיי אדם, כלל פ"ג, סעיף ג', משנה ברורה, סימן תק"ד, ס"ק י"ט.
103. אורח חיים, סימן תק"ד, סעיף א', חיי אדם, כלל פ"ג, סעיפים א', ב', משנה ברורה, סימן תק"ד, ס"ק י"א.
104. משנה ברורה שם, ס"ק י"ט.
105. שבת, דף צ"ג, עמוד ב', במשנה.
106. אורח חיים, סימן ש"ח, סעיף מ"א, מגן אברהם שם, ס"ק ע"א, משנה ברורה שם, ס"ק קנ"ד.
107. פרי מגדים, אשל אברהם, שם, ס"ק ע"א, משנה ברורה שם, ס"ק קנ"ד.
108. שו"ת חלקת יעקב, חלק א', סימן ס"ו.
109. אורח חיים, סימן תקי"ח, סעיף א', מגן אברהם שם, ס"ק א'.
110. אורח חיים, סימן ש"ח, סעיף מ"א, מגן אברהם, שם, ס"ק ע"א, משנה ברורה שם, ס"ק קנ"ד.
111. אורח חיים, סימן שכ"ח, סעיף י"ז ברמ"א.
112. מגן אברהם, סימן שמ"ה, ס"ק ז', ט"ז שם, ס"ק ו'.
113. מגן אברהם, סימן ש"ח, ס"ק ע"א, משנה ברורה שם, ס"ק קנ"ד, שו"ת אגרות משה, אורח חיים, חלק ד', סימן צ"א.
114. אורח חיים, סימן שכ"ח, סעיף י"ז, מגן אברהם, שם, ס"ק י"ד.
115. חיי אדם, כלל ס"ט, סעיף י"ב, משנה ברורה, סימן שכ"ח, ס"ק ק"ב.
116. משנה ברורה, סימן ש"ח, ס"ק קנ"ד.
117. אורח חיים, סימן שכ"ח, סעיף י'.
118. אורח חיים, שם, סעיף י"ז ברמ"א.
119. פרי מגדים, אשל אברהם, סימן ש"ח, ס"ק ע"א, משנה ברורה שם, ס"ק קנ"ד.
120. שמירת שבת כהלכתה, פרק י"ח, סעיף נ"א.
121. משנה ברורה, סימן ש"ח, ס"ק קנ"ג.
122. פרי מגדים, אשל אברהם, סימן שט"ו, ס"ק א', משנה ברורה שם, ס"ק ב'.
123. אורח חיים שם, סעיף ב'.
124. שולחן ערוך הגרש"ז, סימן שט"ו, סעיף ט"ז.
125. שמירת שבת כהלכתה, פרק כ"ד, סעיף י"ד.
126. אורח חיים, סימן שט"ו, סעיף ה', מגן אברהם שם, ס"ק ח'.
127. כף החיים, סימן של"ז, ס"ק ד', שמירת שבת כהלכתה, פרק כ"ח, סעיף מ"ב, הערה צ"ט.
128. אורח חיים, סימן שכ"ח, סעיף ב'.
129. שם, סעיף י"ז.
130. שם, סעיף א'.

131. שם, סעיף י"ז, משנה ברורה שם, ס"ק נ"ח.
132. חיי אדם, כלל ס"ט, סעיף י"ב, משנה ברורה, סימן שכ"ח, ס"ק ק"ב.
133. שו"ת מנחת יצחק, חלק א', סימן ע"ח.
134. אורח חיים, סימן שכ"ח, סעיף א'.
135. שם, סעיף ל"ז.
136. שם, סעיף י"ז, משנה ברורה שם, ס"ק קכ"א.
137. שמירת שבת כהלכתה, פרק ל"ד, סעיף נ"ד.
138. שו"ת אגרות משה, חלק ג', סימן נ"ד.
139. אורח חיים, סימן שכ"ח, סעיף י"ז, משנה ברורה שם, ס"ק קכ"א.
140. מגן אברהם, סימן שכ"ח, ס"ק ל"ב, מחצית השקל שם, משנה ברורה שם, ס"ק פ"ח.
141. שו"ת אגרות משה, אורח חיים, חלק א', סימן קכ"ח, שו"ת מנחת יצחק, חלק ו', סימן קמ"ב.
142. אורח חיים, סימן ש"ו, סעיף ד'.
143. שם.
144. שם, סעיפים ד', ה'.
145. מנחת שבת, סימן צ', ס"ק י"ח, שמירת שבת כהלכתה, פרק כ"ח, סעיף נ"ז.
146. עבודה זרה, דף כ"ב, עמוד א'.
147. יורה דעה, סימן קנ"ג, סעיף ב'.
148. שם, סימן קנ"ד, סעיף א'.
149. מאירי, עבודה זרה, דף כ"ו, עמוד א', שו"ת חות יאיר, סימן ס"ו.
150. תפארת ישראל, עבודה זרה, פרק ב', יכין ס"ק ה', שערים המצויינים בהלכה, סימן קס"ז, ס"ק י"ז.
151. יורה דעה, סימן קנ"ג, סעיף א'.
152. דרכי תשובה שם, ס"ק ד'.
153. סידור הרב יעב"ץ, ערבית לשבת.
154. חיי אדם, כלל קמ"ד, סעיף י"ט.
155. ביאור הלכה, סימן קכ"ח, סעיף א', ד"ה "דזר".

Chapter Eight

Chinuch and Special Children

All parents pray that they will be granted healthy normal children. However, not everyone receives this blessing. Some parents are given special children to raise. These children can be of different types. Some may be mentally retarded, while others can be physically handicapped. Adopted children are also special children in their own way. Each of these categories of children presents specific halalchic problems in regard to chinuch and care. Observant parents given the responsibility of raising such children must be aware of the halachic guidelines ordained by Judaism for doing this task. In addition to the difficult mission of bringing up their children in a general sense, they must also devote attention to raising their special children in accordance with the teachings of Judaism and Halachah.

General Principles

The Talmud states that two categories of adults are exempt from observing mitzvot. These two groups are the deaf mutes and the retarded.[1] Rashi writes that this is true because such individuals have no intelligence.[2] The *Shulchan Aruch* codifies this as binding Halachah. It states that since this is so, these individuals may not be counted towards the ten adult males needed for a minyan.[3]

Children, of course, never have the same personal obligation to observe mitzvot as adults do. Their parents are required, as a result of the duty of chinuch, to train them in the observance of mitzvot. This obligation, as mentioned earlier, does not begin from birth. It starts when the child is intellectually mature enough to understand that a certain action is forbidden or that a specific mitzvah must be performed. Before the child attains this degree of maturity his parents have no obligation of chinuch towards him.[4] The poskim state that parents have no duty of chinuch towards children who are either deaf mutes or mentally retarded. This is because such persons have no intelligence, according to the Talmud, and therefore will never reach the level of maturity needed for chinuch to take place. Moreover, as adults they will have no obligation to fulfill the mitzvot. Thus it makes little sense for parents to have an obligation of chinuch towards them as children.[5]

Despite this, *Peri Megadim* argues that parents do have one requirement towards such children connected with the fulfillment of mitzvot. Just as parents are forbidden, from the time of his birth, to actively cause an infant to sin, so are they prohibited from directly causing a deaf mute or retarded child to violate the Torah from the moment of his birth. In this case, the prohibition does not depend on the intelligence of the child. Parents may not be the active cause of a Jewish child sinning.[6] Some authorities dispute this position, contending that parental involvement of this kind is permitted in regard to special children.[7] The majority of authorities, however, agree with *Peri Megadim* that parents may not be the direct cause of any child violating the Torah.[8]

This means that a parent is not permitted to feed such a child non-kosher food or directly bring him to sin in any other way. On the other hand, if the child does these things on his own the parent is not required to stop him. In addition, the parent certainly has no obligation to see to it that such a child does anything in a positive manner to observe mitzvot.

The Contemporary Deaf-Mute

As mentioned earlier, the whole basis for exempting these two categories of people from mitzvot is the assumption that they possess no intelligence. In contemporary times this assumption has been put into question. It is consequently necessary to modify the preceding statements about deaf mute and mentally retarded children.

In the first place it must be pointed out that the Talmud uses the term deaf-mute in a very specific manner. A person who is deaf but able to speak or mute but able to hear is clearly not included in this category. As long as such an individual has normal intelligence, he is required to observe all the mitzvot in exactly the same way as an ordinary Jew.[9] It is therefore obvious that children who are either deaf or mute are required to be educated, according to the mitzvah of chinuch, just as normal children are. The question only exists in regard to deaf-mute children. In the time of the Talmud it was clearly impossible to educate such children. They consequently grew up ignorant of civilized behavior and could be classified as lacking elementary intelligence. Due to advances in medicine and education in the past two hundred years the situation has totally changed. Today children born with this condition can generally be educated to be productive members of society with an acceptable level of intellectual awareness and intelligence. Parents of deaf-mute children are therefore justified in asking whether the halachic categorization of their offspring as mentally retarded is still relevant today.

The poskim of the past two centuries vigorously debated this question. One school of thought argues that contemporary deaf-mutes who have attended school and learned how to read and write are to be considered as normal Jews in all respects. We assume that such people have full intelligence. This is especially true since they have generally learned how to speak. The fact that they possess the faculty of speech certainly removes them from the talmudic cateogry of deaf-mute. This is so even if they are unable to talk as clearly as other people, as long as their words can be understood.[10]

Other authorities disagree. They contend that whether or not educated deaf-mutes can be considered normal Jews remains an unresolved question. It therefore continues to be unclear whether they are obligated to observe mitzvot or not.[11] A third school of thought maintains that deaf-mutes remain unquestionably free of the requirement to observe the mitzvot no matter what educational attainments they may have achieved.[12]

Contemporary poskim have ruled that an educated deaf-mute who can speak is obligated to observe mitzvot in exactly the same way as any other Jew. His status only remains questionable in regard to certain leniencies which result from this position, such as counting him as part of a minyan. In regard to all other matters, however, he is considered to be the equal of all other Jews.[13] Since this is so, it is obvious that parents have the obligation of chinuch towards such a child in exactly the same manner that they have this requirement towards their other children. No practical difference exists between the two.

The Mentally Deficient

The mentally retarded form the second category of those who are exempt from observing mitzvot. Rashi explains that they are free from this obligation because they lack normal intelligence.[14] A person of this type is referred to by the halachic term *shoteh*. Parents have no responsibility of chinuch towards children who fall into this category. *Peri Megadim* explains why this is so. He states that since these children will never reach the level of maturity needed to perform mitzvot, chinuch does not apply to them.[15] As mentioned previously, according to most opinions, parents are forbidden to actively cause such children to sin by feeding them non-kosher food or by directly influencing them to violate any other prohibition.[16] There is, however, no parental obligation to stop them from doing any forbidden act on their own volition. There is also no requirement for parents to educate children of this type in the positive fulfillment of mitzvot.[17] It should, however, be noted that a *shoteh* is considered to be a full Jew in other respects, despite his being exempt from the requirement to observe mitzvot. Such a child or adult has a Jewish soul, just as every Jew does. It goes without saying that his life is as precious as that of anyone else. He may not be harmed or hurt in any way.[18]

A tremendous number of variations exist in regard to mental retardation. The degree of retardation involved often differs drastically from one case to another. A whole spectrum of lower than normal intelligence exits. At one end of the range are people with an intellectual level only slightly below what is considered to be normal. At the other end individuals with extremely severe forms of retardation can be found. It must be stressed that not everyone considered mentally retarded by contemporary standards fits into the halachic category of *shoteh*. Parents who have children with mild forms of retardation are in many cases obligated to fulfill the duty of chinuch towards them.

The *Shulchan Aruch* states that individuals who are not as sharp or as apt as the average person cannot be placed in the category of *shoteh*. Such people are required to observe mitzvot just as other Jews are. They may, therefore, be counted towards a minyan or towards the number of people needed to say the Birchat Hamazon as a public prayer.[19] This is true even though the average person considers such individuals to be retarded. Since they have a modicum of intelligence they cannot be halachically defined as belonging to the class of *shoteh*.[20] Later poskim point out that parents are required to educate children who possess minimal intelligence and bring them up to observe all the mitzvot. The duty of chinuch applies to these children just as it does to other children.[21]

It is clear that so many shadings of retardation exist that it is impossible to clearly delineate, in a work such as this, at what point a child is deemed to be so lacking in intellect that his parents are free of the obligation of teaching him to observe mitzvot. Obviously, expert rabbinic guidance must be sought in this area on a case-by-case basis. It also must be borne in mind that in many instances modern methods of education can succeed in so raising the intelligence level of a special child that he can be placed in the category of the average Jew. When this happens, parents

Chinuch and Special Children 143

are clearly required by their responsibility of chinuch to educate such a child to fulfill all the mitzvot.[22] Modern poskim agree that if a special child has the potential to achieve the intellectual level of an average six-year-old, his parents have the clear obligation to train him to observe mitzvot. Upon reaching bar or bat mitzvah such a child will be obligated to observe all the mitzvot just as an ordinary Jewish adult must. If, however, he or she can never reach even this level of maturity no chinuch requirements exist.[23]

Parents often find it necessary to consider placing retarded children into special institutions which can care for them. These institutions generally are not Jewish in nature, and halachic requirements, such as kosher food, are not observed. If the child in question is below normal in mentality but not considered a *shoteh*, it is clear that there is no permissibility for parents to send him to such an institution. When parents do this, they definitely violate their responsibility of chinuch. That duty obligates them to train their children to observe mitzvot and make sure that they commit no infractions of Halachah. Obviously, these obligations cannot be fulfilled in such an environment.[24]

The more common case, however, involves sending a child, who is so retarded that he clearly is a shoteh to this type of an institution or school. As mentioned earlier, parents are not required to train this kind of child to observe mitzvot, since chinuch does not apply to him. Despite this, parents are forbidden to cause a child who is a shoteh to sin. It would appear that by placing a child in this type of living arrangement parents are indeed causing their child to violate Halachah. This is because it is known beforehand that only non-kosher food will be served in the institution. This seemingly should be forbidden. It is obvious that if this is the case, great hardships would result for the parents of retarded children. They would have to keep the children at home or provide a Jewish institution for them. Often, neither of these alternatives is possible.

Chatam Sofer argues that parents commit no real violation of Halachah by sending severely retarded children to such institutions. When parents do so, they do not directly feed non-kosher food to their child but cause this to happen indirectly. This, he concludes, is permissible. He adds, however, that once the child becomes bar mitzvah he should be removed from the institution. Rabbi Sofer then goes on to state that while this is all true from the standpoint of strict Jewish law, parents should still not follow this course of action. Non-kosher food, he writes, has a degrading influence on the soul and parents should not corrupt their innocent child's soul in the eyes of God.[25]

Rabbi Moshe Feinstein discusses this same question. He agrees with Chatam Sofer that parents commit no violation of Halachah by placing children in such institutions. In this case they are only the indirect cause of their children consuming non-kosher food, rather than the direct agents responsible for this action. He adds that since an adult shoteh is also not obligated to observe mitzvot there is no requirement to remove the child from the institutional setting even after bar mitzvah or bat mitzvah. Rabbi Feinstein concludes, unlike Chatam Sofer, that placing such children in institutions cannot be condemned because of the effect non-kosher food has on the soul. Only if the school in question is able to raise the mental level of the child so that he will no longer be considered a shoteh can such an argument be made. However, if the child will continue to be a shoteh no such objection exists. He, therefore, permits parents to choose institutionalization or living at a non-Jewish residential facility for their children in these kinds of cases.[26]

Adopted Children

Adopted children form another category of special children. They are no different from all other boys and girls in their physical or mental abilities, but do differ from them in the nature of their origin. This is because they are not the biological descendants of their parents, but rather the offspring of others who have been accepted as children by their adoptive parents. There are various halachic issues created by the raising of adopted children. Since this is an increasing fact of life in the contemporary Jewish community, these questions must be discussed.

The actual fact of adopting children carries with it various halachic problems. This is true whether the child to be adopted is of Jewish origin or not. It is not within the purview of a work such as this to address these problems. We will instead concentrate on the issues of chinuch for such children once they have been adopted and the halachic complications related to their care.

It is important to note that from the standpoint of Halachah, adopting a child who has no one to care for him and raising him to adulthood is considered to be a most lofty mitzvah. The Talmud states that he who raises an orphan in his home performs a most meritorious act. It goes on to say that when a person does this, the child involved is considered as if he were the natural-born son or daughter of his benefactors.[27] Some poskim extend this to mean that a childless couple who raise such children are considered to have thereby fulfilled the mitzvah of giving birth to children.[28]

Nevertheless, it must be stated that there is a fundamental difference between Halachah and secular law on the subject of adoption. Secular law envisions the possibility of a child not biologically related to his adoptive parent becoming the son or daughter of that parent with all the rights and responsibilities of a natural-born child. Halachah does not accept this position. Full kinship, in the sense of a parent-child relationship, can only be established by the fact of birth. An adopted child cannot halachically be considered completely the same as a natural one, either in regard to the halachic obligations of parents to children or in connection with the responsibilities of children to their parents.[29]

The obligations of parents to children include, as mentioned in the earlier chapters of this work, caring for the child and providing food and clothing. A parent who refuses to do this can be forced by a Jewish court to provide these necessities.[30] It would seem that since an adopted child is not a biological descendant of his adoptive parent, no such obligation can be imposed on the parent. In other words, if an adoptive parent refuses, subsequent to the adoption, to feed or clothe an adopted child, there is no halachic basis on which to force the parent to do these things. Technically speaking, the adopted child is a total stranger to the parent. While it is a mitzvah to care for such a child, there appears to be no mandatory requirement to do so.

The same would seem to be true of the obligations of chinuch. Halachah imposes the requirement of training a child to observe mitzvot on the child's biological parents. Other Jewish adults are not permitted to directly cause a child to sin, but they are not required to stop the child from sinning on his own. Unrelated adults are certainly not obligated to see to it that the child observes mitzvot in a positive fashion.[31] Since from a halachic standpoint an adopted child does not become the full equivalent of a natural child, it would appear that adoptive parents are not bound by the rules of chinuch in the same way that biological parents are.

Rabbi Ben Zion Uziel argues that these assumptions are false. He cites the *Shulchan Aruch*'s recognition that a person can voluntarily assume the obligations of caring for a stranger. Once someone does this he is halachically bound to fulfill his commitment and cannot free himself of it. The same is true, Rabbi Uziel concludes, of an adoptive parent. By accepting the adopted child as his own, he has made a binding promise to do everything for that child which Halachah requires a biological parent to do. His obligations towards the child are identical to those of any other parent in all details. This includes caring for the material needs of the child, teaching him Torah, and training him to observe mitzvot.[32] This position is accepted by most contemporary poskim.[33]

Even though adopted children are considered to be equal to natural children in regard to these matters, one further question remains. Every child is given a legal Jewish title consisting of his or her Hebrew name followed by the words "son of" or "daughter of" and their father's name. This title is used when the children are first named and later when men are called up to the

Torah and when Mi Sheberach prayers are recited. It is also used for the ketubah (marriage contract), the get (writ of divorce), and other halachic documents. The question is whether the name of adoptive father can be part of an adopted child's title for such purposes. After all, since an adopted child is not physically the offspring of the adoptive parent, the use of such a phrase would appear to be an act of fraud.

Rabbi Moshe Feinstein argues that it is permitted to refer to an adopted child as son or daughter of his adoptive parent when the child is named or later called to the Torah. He states that one may call a person by the name of the person who raises him without fear of any halachic impropriety.[34] Most other contemporary poskim concur.[35] The question of what name to use in a ketubah or get is much more complicated and lies beyond the scope of this work.

There is one last halachic issue involved with the care of adopted children. As mentioned earlier, the prohibition of yichud forbids a member of one sex to be alone with a member of the opposite sex in a situation where they have completely uninterrupted privacy. This is due to the fear of something immoral occuring. Yichud applies to females once they reach the age of three and males at the age of nine.[36] Parents and children are normally exempted from this prohibition. The biological bond between them is considered to be so strong that a father may be alone with his daughter or a mother with her son under all circumstances.[37] It is similarly forbidden for members of one sex to kiss or embrace members of the other sex outside of a marriage relationship.[38] Again, parents and children are exempted from this prohibition. There is no halachic limitation on expressions of affection between them.[39]

The question, however, remains whether these exemptions hold true for adopted children and adoptive parents. Many poskim argue that both yichud and physical expressions of affection are forbidden between adoptive parents and adopted children of the opposite sex. Since they are not biologically related, they must be considered no different than strangers in regard to these prohibitions. This would mean that a father would be forbidden from embracing, kissing, or being alone with an adopted daughter who is past the age of three. A mother would similarly be prohibited from any of these activities involving an adopted son who is older than nine.[40]

Other poskim disagree, stating that the emotional bond created by adoption is so strong that it can be considered the equal of biological birth in regard to these matters. Those who hold this view allow adoptive parents to be alone with the adopted children of the opposite sex and show them physical signs of affection in exactly the same way that natural parents are allowed to do this. Some authorities maintain that this holds only as long as the children do not know that they are adopted, but once they learn the truth it is no longer permitted, for then we are forced to consider them as strangers.[41] Others hold that even after the children know of their origin the parents are allowed to behave in this manner. However, even the most lenient opinion does not permit such activities between adopted siblings. Only parents and adopted children may behave in this manner. Since the parents have brought up the children from infancy they may, according to these poskim, rely on the emotional bond which has been created between them. The bond is sufficient to permit yichud and affectionate behavior between adopted children and their adoptive parents.[42]

Notes

1. חגיגה, דף ג', עמוד א'.
2. שם, דף ב', עמוד א', רש"י ד"ה „חוץ מחרש".
3. אורח חיים, סימן נ"ה, סעיף ח'.
4. משנה ברורה, סימן שמ"ג, ס"ק ג'.
5. פרי מגדים, פתיחה כוללת לאורח חיים, חלק ב', ס"ק א', ט', משבצות זהב, אורח חיים, סימן רס"ו, ס"ק ד'.
6. פרי מגדים, פתיחה כוללת לאורח חיים, חלק ב', ס"ק א'.
7. שו"ת שיבת ציון, סימן ד'.

8. שו"ת חתם סופר, אורח חיים, סימן פ"ג, שדי חמד, מערכת ח', כלל קט"ו.
9. אורח חיים, סימן נ"ה, סעיף ח', פרי מגדים, פתיחה כוללת לאורח חיים, חלק ב', ס"ק ה'.
10. שו"ת מהרש"ם, חלק ב', סימן ק"מ, שו"ת בית שלמה, אורח חיים, סימן צ"ה.
11. שו"ת דברי חיים, אבן העזר, חלק ב', סימן ע"ב, שו"ת מהר"ם שיק, אבן העזר, סימן ע"ט.
12. שו"ת זכר שמחה, סימן ט'.
13. שו"ת היכל יצחק, אבן העזר, חלק ב', סימן מ"ז, שו"ת יחוה דעת, חלק ב', סימן ו', מנחת שלמה, סימן ל"ד.
14. חגיגה, דף ב', עמוד א', רש"י שם, ד"ה "חוץ מחרש".
15. פרי מגדים, פתיחה כוללת לאורח חיים, חלק ב', ס"ק א', ט'.
16. שדי חמד, מערכת ח', כלל קט"ו.
17. פרי מגדים, פתיחה כוללת לאורח חיים, חלק ב', ס"ק א', ט', משבצות זהב, אורח חיים, סימן רס"ו, ס"ק ד'.
18. שו"ת מהרי"ל, סימן קצ"ו, פרי מגדים, פתיחה כוללת לאורח חיים, חלק ב', ס"ק א'.
19. אורח חיים, סימן קצ"ט, סעיף י', מגן אברהם שם, ס"ק ח'.
20. משנה ברורה שם, ס"ק כ"ט.
21. שו"ת אגרות משה, אורח חיים, חלק ב', סימן פ"ח, יורה דעה, חלק ב', סימן נ"ט.
22. שם.
23. מנחת שלמה, סימן ל"ד, תשובת הגר"מ פיינשטיין בחוברת עם התורה, מהדורא ב', חוברת ב'.
24. שו"ת אגרות משה, יורה דעה, חלק ב', סימן נ"ט.
25. שו"ת חתם סופר, אורח חיים, סימן פ"ג.
26. שו"ת אגרות משה, אורח חיים, חלק ב', סימן פ"ח.
27. סנהדרין, דף ט', עמוד ב'.
28. חכמת שלמה, אבן העזר, סימן א', ס"ק א'.
29. ספר ליקוטי מאיר, פרק א', סימן ב'.
30. אבן העזר, סימן ע"א, סעיף א', סימן ע"ג, סעיף ו'.
31. אורח חיים, סימן שמ"ג, משנה ברורה שם, ס"ק א', ד'.
32. שערי עוזיאל, חלק ב', שער ל"ט, פרק א', ס"ק ג', ז'.
33. נחלת צבי, חלק א', עמוד ל"ה, ליקוטי מאיר, פרק י"ח, סימן א'.
34. שו"ת אגרות משה, יורה דעה, חלק א', סימן קס"א.
35. ליקוטי מאיר, פרק ד'.
36. אבן העזר, סימן כ"ב, סעיף י"א.
37. שם, סעיף א'.
38. אבן העזר, סימן כ"א, סעיף ז'.
39. שם.
40. שו"ת מנחת יצחק, חלק ד', סימן מ"ט.
41. שו"ת ציץ אליעזר, חלק ו', סימן מ', פרק כ"א.
42. שו"ת עשה לך רב, חלק ג', סימן ל"ט.

Chapter Nine
Bar and Bat Mitzvah

Parents are bound by the duty of chincuh to see to it that their children are trained to observe mitzvot while they are minors. The purpose of doing this is to ensure that the children will continue to be religiously observant Jews after they become adults. Once children attain adulthood, making certain that they obey all of the mitzvot of the Torah is no longer the responsibility of their parents. From that point on the former child is now a halachic adult and therefore required to follow God's laws in his or her own right. In this sense the responsibility of chinuch by parents comes to an end once their children arrive at the age of adulthood. The attainment of this important milestone in life is accompanied by various halachic rules and practices. In order to correctly end their duty of chinuch parents must be familiar with these important guidelines and laws.

Halachic Adulthood

Jewish law gives one age for adulthood in regard to males and another in reference to females. The Mishnah tells us that a person becomes fully obligated to observe all mitzvot at the age of thirteen.[1] The Talmud elsewhere explains that this refers to a male. A female, on the other hand, reaches halachic maturity at the age of twelve. This means that once boys get to their thirteenth birthday and once girls attain their twelfth birthday they are to be considered as full adults in the eyes of Halachah. They are bound by all the obligations and responsibilities which govern other adult Jews. It is for this reason that a boy becomes bar mitzvah at thirteen and a girl becomes bat mitzvah at twelve.[2]

This does not mean that age alone is the sole determinant of whether a child has attained halachic adulthood or not. For matters involving questions of Torah law, additional evidence of physical maturity is generally required before a child can definitively said to be an adult. Such evidence is provided by the appearance of a minimum of two public hairs on the body after the age of adulthood has been reached.[3] However, for issues of rabbinic law we rely on age alone as proof of adulthood. Once a child has reached the specified age, it is justifiable to assume that he or she is physically mature and therefore a full halachic adult in these matters.[4] Even when a question of Torah law is involved we rely on age alone as evidence of adulthood when doing so causes a stringency rather than a leniency for the individual concerned.[5]

The practical result of these rules is that a boy who has reached the age of thirteen may be counted in a minyan or be given an aliyah to the Torah. Since these matters involve rabbinic law, no further evidence of maturity is required.[6] Similarly, boys who are thirteen years of age and girls who are twelve are required to fast on Yom Kippur without any further evidence of physical maturity. This is because fasting on Yom Kippur is mandated by Torah law. Refusing to rely on age alone in this case would result in a leniency, for the children involved would be excused from fasting unless evidence of physical maturity was available. In such a situation, we accept age by itself as an indication of adulthood in order to give the children the added stringency of observing mitzvot just as all adults do.[7]

This pattern applies to most mitzvot and laws. There are, however, exceptions. For example, we do not accept a boy even above the age of thirteen as an adult to write tefillin or Torah scrolls. Physical evidence of maturity is needed in this case, because relying on age alone would create a halachic leniency. It is a matter of Torah law that for tefillin to be kosher they must be written by an adult. If tefillin written by a boy were accepted, without further proof that he is indeed an adult, a violation of Torah law might occur.[8] As a practical matter, most poskim accept a full growth of facial hair on the beard as reliable proof of physical maturity in this case. When this exists, we accept the individual involved as halachically qualified to perform these tasks.[9]

Adulthood and Bar and Bat Mitzvah

Halachic works do not state anywhere why thirteen should be regarded as the age of adulthood for boys and twelve for girls. Both Rashi[10] and Rabbenu Asher[11] state that the designation of these ages is a result of a direct tradition going back to Mount Sinai with no specific textual basis in Scripture or logical explanation. Midrashic sources do, however, supply reasons for these choices. They state that thirteen is the crucial age of decision-making for young men. The two brothers Jacob and Esau, were indistinguishable in their life-styles until that age. Once they reached this point, their future tendencies in life were revealed. Jacob began to devote himself to the study of Torah, while Esau became an outright idol worshipper.[12] Another Midrash says that until the age of thirteen a child only possesses the evil inclination which leads him to sin. Once he reaches the age of bar mitzvah, however, he receives his yetzer tov, the good inclination, as well. In other words, his capacity to do good and evil and to be responsible for his actions is only achieved at that stage of life.[13] A third Midrash similarly tells us that Abraham categorically rejected the idol worship of his father Terach when he reached the age of thirteen.[14] This is again confirmation for the fact that intellectual and religious maturity is reached by males at that age. Obviously, all this would be true for girls when they become bat mitzvah at twelve.

The Date of the Bar or Bat Mitzvah

It might seem to be an easy matter for parents to calculate the date of their child's bar mitzvah or bat mitzvah. In most cases no complicated questions come up. One merely follows his child's birthday in calculating the date of the bar or bat mitzvah. In certain specific cases, however, various issues need to be clarified in order to do this correctly.

A boy becomes bar mitzvah and a girl becomes bat mitzvah when they fully attain the ages of thirteen and twelve respectively. This means that when their thirteenth or twelfth Hebrew birth date arrives they become adults in the eyes of Halachah. The child becomes an adult as soon as his or her birthday begins, which occurs, as far as Jewish law is concerned, with the nightfall of the previous day, since according to the Jewish calendar the night is always a part of the following day. This rule applies regardless of the time of day of the child's birth on the same date twelve or thirteen years earlier. It is not necessary to wait until the particular minute at which he was born in order to recognize him as an adult. Once the day has begun, the child is considered a full adult by Jewish law.[15]

One exception to this rule occurs in regard to a child born during twilight. Since Halachah regards it as unclear whether twilight is part of the preceding day or the next day, a child born during this time must wait until the next day before being granted the status of a Jewish adult.[16] Furthermore, the child's thirteenth or twelfth birthday must have actually begun for him or her to be considered an adult. If the date falls on a Shabbat this can cause a problem. It is customary in many communities to begin the Sabbath early and to recite the Maariv prayer on Friday evening before the time of actual nightfall. When this is done, a bar mitzvah boy whose birthday falls on the Sabbath may not serve as chazzan for Maariv because he only becomes an adult at nightfall and the prayer is being recited before that time.[17]

A further problem in calculating the date of bar or bat mitzvah occurs in relation to a leap year. A Jewish leap year has an additional thirteenth month added to it. This month, known as Adar I, is inserted into the calendar between the months of Shevat and Adar II. Parents of a child born in the month of Adar are faced with the problem of calculating the date of their child's adulthood when a leap year is involved. This can occur because the child was born in a leap year or because his twelfth or thirteenth birthday occurs in a leap year. The question obviously is which month to consider correct for calculating the bar or bat mitzvah date.

Most poskim agree that if the child was born in a leap year and his or her bar or bat mitzvah also occurs in a leap year, the actual birth date should be followed. In other words, if the child was born in the first month of Adar his adulthood begins on the same date in that month, while if the birth occurred in the second month of Adar that month should be followed when calculating the bar or bat mitzvah day.

However, when the child was born in a leap year, but the year of the twelfth or thirteenth birthday contains only one month of Adar, the date can only be calculated according to that one month. This means that in a leap year a child born on the twenty-ninth of Adar II becomes an adult on the twenty-ninth of Adar, while another child, born in the same year, on the first of Adar II, becomes an adult on the first of Adar. Paradoxically, the younger child becomes an adult before the older one.

The third possible case occurs when a child was born in a year with only one month of Adar, but the year of adulthood, as a leap year, contains two months of Adar. In this case the bar or bat mitzvah is celebrated in the second month of Adar. This is because the bar or bat mitzvah must be observed in Adar, and Adar II is not considered to the real month of Adar. It is merely an extra month inserted into the calendar to make the year into a leap year.[18]

Bar Mitzvah Ceremony

As far as strict Halachah is concerned, a boy automatically becomes bar mitzvah when he reaches the age of thirteen. No ceremony or special action is necessary for him to enter into the state of adulthood. He simply becomes a Jewish adult by reaching the required age. Despite this, universal Jewish custom, or minhag, has established a specific way to mark this important occasion in a boy's life. The bar mitzvah boy is given an aliyah to the Torah, thus publicizing his emergence as a Jewish adult.[19] Since according to contemporary practice a minor boy is never given an aliyah, the calling of the bar mitzvah boy to the Torah makes it evident to all that he has become an adult.[20] The custom of giving an aliyah to a boy becoming bar mitzvah is so strong that he has precedence in being called to the Torah over all others except for a groom who is either about to be married or was just married in the previous week.[21] It should be noted that the bar mitzvah boy is only entitled to such preference when his bar mitzvah ceremony is being held in the actual week of his thirteenth birthday. If, however, it is held at a different time, other people, such as those who are observing a yahrzeit that week, have precedence over the bar mitzvah boy.[22] Of course, it is usually possible to arrange matters so that the boy celebrating his bar mitzvah receives an aliyah to the Torah under all circumstances.

It should be noted that it is nowhere specified what the aliyah given to the bar mitzvah boy should be. It is certainly not necessary to call him for Maftir. Any aliyah is satisfactory. According to some opinions, the boy can be given his aliyah on a weekday just as well as on Shabbat.[23] *Magen Avraham*, however, states that the accepted minhag is for the bar mitzvah aliyah to be given specifically on a Shabbat rather than a weekday.[24] Later poskim quote this statement of the *Magen Avraham* as the basis for normative procedure.[25]

Rema states that the father of a bar mitzvah boy is required to make a special berachah at the time that his son receives his aliyah to the Torah. This berachah is known as Baruch Shepatrani. *Magen Avraham* explains that the purpose of this blessing is for the father to thank God that he is no longer responsible for his son's sins. Until the bar mitzvah the father is bound by the duty of chinuch to see to it that his son does not sin. Now that his son is an adult that responsibility is gone.[26] Rabbi Mordechai Yaffe explains the belssing differently. He writes that with this berachah the father thanks God for having freed his son from being punished for the father's sins. This is based on the idea that minors can be punished for the sins of their parents. Now that the son is an adult he is no longer liable to such punishment.[27]

Rema continues by saying that a father should leave out any mention of God's name and His sovereignty when reciting this berachah. Since this blessing is not mentioned in the Talmud, it is questionable whether a father is actually required to recite it. Whenever it is doubtful whether or not a blessing should be made, God's name and His sovereignty are omitted from the berachah.[28] Later authorities disagree with Rema on this issue. They state that a father should make this berachah in the normal way, using God's name and referring to His rulership over the world. This can be done because the berachah is mentioned in Midrashic literature and can therefore be considered binding on the father of a bar mitzvah boy.[29] Some poskim decide in accordance with Rema,[30] but the majority seem to disagree with him and prescribe that the berachah be recited in the normal way.[31]

Magen Avraham states that parents are required to make a feast in honor of the bar mitzvah of their son. This meal is considered to be a seudat mitzvah, a feast made in fulfillment of a mitzvah. To properly do this, he continues, the meal should be made on the boy's actual thirteenth birthday. After all, it is on that day that he becomes obligated to observe all mitzvot as an adult. Nevertheless, he concludes, parents can also fulfill this obligation on a day which is not the boy's actual birthday. As long as the bar mitzvah boy gives a speech containing words of Torah, the occasion is transformed into a full seudat mitzvah.[32]

Bat Mitzvah

A girl becomes a Jewish adult when she reaches the age of twelve. At that time, the girl becomes bat mitzvah. As such, she is now required to observe all the laws which bind an adult Jewish woman. A girl automatically becomes bat mitzvah when she reaches this age, exactly in the same way that a boy becomes bar mitzvah. No ceremony is required for her to achieve this change in her legal status. She simply becomes an adult with the passing of time and the maturing of her body.

Historically no ceremony was accepted to mark a girl's bat mitzvah. She merely reached her adulthood without much fuss or fanfare. Despite this, contemporary parents often express the desire that something of a formal nature be done to take note of this important occasion in their daughter's life. The girl herself, too, often is desirous of such an event being held. These people are aware that Jewish law and custom do not prescribe anything of this nature for a bat mitzvah. Nevertheless, they wish to know if it is permissible or praiseworthy to voluntarily take notice of this important event in a girl's life.

It is obvious that a bat mitzvah girl cannot be given an aliyah to the Torah to mark her coming of age as is done with a bar mitzvah boy. This is because women cannot receive such synagogue honors.[33] There are parents, however, who wish to have the bat mitzvah celebrated in the synagogue in some form. For example, the girl might address the congregation or receive a bat mitzvah present there. There seems to be no halachic prohibition on ceremonies of this kind. Despite this, Rabbi Moshe Feinstein argues that it is forbidden to hold such activities within the precincts of a synagogue. He writes that since Halachah does not demand a bat mitzvah ceremony, such actions must be considered purely voluntary in nature rather than mitzvah-prescribed. These ceremonies as such have no mitzvah value. They detract from the sanctity due to a synagogue and cannot be held there. Rabbi Feinstein concludes that if the family wishes to hold a gathering at home to mark the occasion it is totally permissible to do so.[34] Rabbi Yechiel Weinberg disagrees. He states that a bat mitzvah ceremony does indeed have Torah value in today's society. The ritual marking of a girl's Jewish adulthood has an important effect in strengthening her dedication towards living a life of Torah and mitzvot. He concludes that such ceremonies should be encouraged. They should, however, not be held in the synagogue sanctuary itself, but rather in the hall or some other room of the synagogue.[35]

Many authorities agree that parents should hold a festive meal to mark their daughter's bat mitzvah just as they would for a boy's bar mitzvah. The meal is to be considered a seudat mitzvah in the same way that a bar mitzvah dinner is given this status.[36] Others note that the prevailing custom is not to hold such a feast in honor of a bat mitzvah. They, however, still consider it to be appropriate for the day to be marked in some special way.[37] Rabbi Moshe Feinstein is of the opinion that any celebration associated with a bat mitzvah is of a voluntary nature. A meal held in honor of the occasion is, according to his view, not a seudat mitzvah, and there is no halachic imperative to hold a special event of any type to mark this occasion.[38]

A bar mitzvah is, of course the time at which the blessing of Baruch Shepatrani is called for. Halachic authorities are virtually unanimous in agreeing that this blessing should not be made when a girl reaches her twelfth birthday. Different reasons are given for this. *Peri Megadim* explains that since there are fewer mitzvot which parents must train a girl to observe, there is no need to make this blessing when a girl becomes an adult.[39] Other authorities state that Baruch Shepatrani is only called for when there is a duty to teach a child Torah. Since women are exempt from this requirement, the berachah is not made at the time a girl becomes bat mitzvah.[40]

Conclusion

It is undoubtedly true that boys become Jewish adults at the age of thirteen and girls at the age of twelve. Once they reach these ages, they are no longer considered children in regard to the parental obligation of chinuch. They themselves rather than their parents, are now responsible for their actions as religious Jews. Despite this, parents are still obligated to influence and teach their children in regard to mitzvah observance long after they have reached bar mitzvah or bat mitzvah age. Parents no longer have the primary responsibility to see that this happens, but they still retain a secondary obligation along these lines. The *Shulchan Aruch* states that a parent is required to observe the actions of his grown children and to try to stop them from doing wrong. If he is capable of doing this and does not attempt to, he is considered to be a sinner in his own right.[41] Later poskim take the same position.[42] This thought should serve to remind us that the parental duty of chinuch, at least in its broader sense, is one which continues throughout the lifetime of every parent and every child. It is a God-given part of the all-important relationship that exists between parents and their children.

Notes

1. אבות, פרק ה', משנה כ"ד.
2. מסכת יומא, דף פ"ב, עמוד א'.
3. אורח חיים, סימן נ"ה, סעיף ה'.
4. שם, מגן אברהם שם, ס"ק ז', משנה ברורה שם, ס"ק ל"א.
5. אורח חיים, סימן ל"ז, סעיף ג', פרי מגדים, אשל אברהם שם, ס"ק ד'.
6. משנה ברורה, סימן נ"ה, ס"ק ל"א.
7. אורח חיים, סימן תרט"ז, סעיף ב', מגן אברהם שם, ס"ק ג'.
8. אורח חיים, סימן ל"ט, סעיף א', מגן אברהם שם, ס"ק א'.
9. משנה ברורה שם, ס"ק ג', ביאור הלכה שם, ד"ה „או קטן".
10. רש"י, ד"ה „בן י"ג", אבות, פרק ה', משנה כ"ד.
11. שו"ת הרא"ש, כלל ט"ז, סימן א'.
12. בראשית רבה, ס"ג, י'.
13. אבות דרבי נתן, פרק ט"ז, משנה ב'.
14. פרקי דרבי אליעזר, פרק כ"ו.
15. משנה ברורה, סימן נ"ה, ס"ק מ"ב.
16. שם.
17. אורח חיים, סימן נ"ג, סעיף י', מגן אברהם, שם, ס"ק י"ג.
18. אורח חיים, סימן נ"ה, סעיף י', חיי אדם, כלל ס"ו, סעיף א', משנה ברורה סימן נ"ה, ס"ק מ"ג, מ"ד, מ"ה.
19. מגן אברהם, סימן רכ"ה, ס"ק ד'.

20. משנה ברורה, שער הציון שם, ס"ק ז'.
21. שערי אפרים, שער ב', סעיף א'.
22. שם, סעיף י'.
23. שם.
24. מגן אברהם, סימן רכ"ה, ס"ק ד'.
25. משנה ברורה שם, ס"ק ו', כף החיים שם, ס"ק י'.
26. מגן אברהם שם, ס"ק ה'.
27. לבוש שם, ס"ק ב'.
28. דרכי משה שם, ס"ק א'.
29. ביאור הגר"א שם, ד"ה „יש אומרים", חיי אדם, כלל ס"ה, סעיף ג'.
30. כף החיים, אורח חיים, סימן רכ"ה, ס"ק ט"ז.
31. משנה ברורה שם, ס"ק ח', קיצור שולחן ערוך, סימן ס"א, סעיף ח'.
32. מגן אברהם שם, ס"ק ד'.
33. אורח חיים, סימן רפ"ב, סעיף ג'.
34. שו"ת אגרות משה, חלק א', סימן ק"ד.
35. שו"ת שרידי אש, חלק ג', סימן צ"ג.
36. שו"ת עשה לך רב, חלק א', סימן ל"א, שו"ת יין הטוב, חלק ב', סימן ו'.
37. בן איש חי, חלק א', ראה, אות י"ז.
38. שו"ת אגרות משה, אורח חיים, חלק א', סימן ק"ד.
39. פרי מגדים, אשל אברהם, אורח חיים, סימן רכ"ה, ס"ק ה'.
40. שו"ת עשה לך רב, חלק א', סימן ל"א.
41. אבן העזר, סימן קע"ח, סעיף כ"א.
42. משנה ברורה, סימן רכ"ה, ס"ק ז'.